LIFE MASTERY

PERSONAL PROGRESSION TOWARD
AN INFINITE POTENTIAL

SHERRY STIRLING FERNANDEZ

ISBN: 978-1-951503-41-3 (Hardcover)
ISBN: 978-1-951503-42-0 (Paperback)

DEDICATION

To Christopher, Merry, Andrew, Katie, Sarah, and Summer—
my six marvelous children who helped me understand
the infinite potential of a human being.
Each of them is my everything.

CONTENTS

INTRODUCTION

In 1990, collective farming was dismantled in Vietnam, and for the first time, Vietnamese families were able to farm their own land. Unfortunately, it wasn't all good news. They had lost farming support systems from the Soviet Union, and typhoons had been relentless. Without government subsidies to feed their families, 65% of children under the age of five were suffering from malnutrition. Save the Children, a humanitarian organization for children, sent Jerry Sternin to Vietnam to find a solution. Sternin did not speak Vietnamese, he had no funding, and little government support. The situation was overwhelming, but his solution was brilliant.

Sternin searched for and found families where the children were thriving rather than starving, even though they had no more financial means than the other villagers. He visited those families at mealtimes to see what they did differently. He discovered that the mothers of the thriving children were gathering tiny shrimps, crabs, and snails from the rice paddies and cooking them, along with sweet potato greens, into their children's food. While this was not a common custom in Vietnam, adding these items gave the children vital nutrition.

Sternin had found a sustainable solution to the plague of malnutrition, and it was within reach of every family. He could have chosen to play the hero by using his expert status to teach the villagers how to save their children. Instead, Sternin did something much wiser—he recognized the real experts were the Vietnamese mothers who had already found a way to nourish their children and had been *practicing certain principles with success*. Sternin recruited and organized the mothers of the thriving children to teach those who had not yet discovered how to do it on their own. The mothers met in local huts and cooked together. Vietnamese mothers became *authorities* as they taught what they knew to other mothers, and those other mothers then became *authorities* as well. In village after village, these mothers taught each other how to reduce malnutrition and provide better nutrition to their children.

Those mothers in Vietnam did not need a degree in nutrition to be *authorities*. Their successful living by certain principles made them experts among their peers. Like those Vietnamese mothers, my own *authority* does not come from *expert status*, a degree, or courses I have taken, but from a lifetime of learning and *practicing certain principles with success*. The success derived from applying those principles is as available as shrimps and sweet potato greens were to Vietnamese mothers in 1990.

A lifetime of learning, practicing, refining, and teaching certain skills has given me the privilege of being a role model for those who follow. Willie Nelson sings, "I have a couple of years on you, babe, that's all." My advantage is having a couple more years of practice, that's all. As you attain success from applying these principles, you also have an obligation to share them, and as you do, you will become an authority in your circle of influence. You might even say to someone, someday, "I have a couple of years on you, that's all." At least, that is how it works in the song.

PART I

WHY

The great fire of 1666 leveled London. The world-famous architect, Christopher Wren, was commissioned to rebuild St Paul's Cathedral. There is an oft-repeated story about a day in 1671 when Wren observed three bricklayers. Wren asked them, "What are you doing?" to which the first bricklayer replied, "I'm a bricklayer. I'm working hard laying bricks to feed my family." The second bricklayer responded, "I'm a builder. I'm building a wall." But the third bricklayer, the most passionate and committed of the group, said, "I'm a cathedral builder. I'm building a great cathedral to the Almighty."

Questions such as "What is your why?" or advice like "Start with why" are trendy right now. I like this kind of conversation because knowing the *why* behind any decision refines the commitment to that decision. That is why Friedrich Nietzsche said, "He who has a *why* to live for can bear almost any how." Knowing your *why* is the critical first step in figuring out how to achieve the goals that excite you and create a life where you thrive rather than just survive. When you know your *why*, you will find the courage to take the risks you will need to take, stay motivated when adversity strikes, and maintain a clear sense of purpose. Doing so will enable you to live a life that exceeds your dreams.

Like the bricklayers, each of us is building something that has the potential to be spectacular and leave an enduring legacy. We are building a life. The life we are building is our own masterpiece on the only canvas we have. The quality of your masterpiece is determined by your *why*. What is your *why*? It is your own particular passions, desires, dreams, life mission, and the people you love.

My husband is a great letter writer. He has a way of expressing his love for people in writing that makes any letter you get from him a treasure. After he wrote a letter to one of our granddaughters, Lilly, who was twelve at the time, he received a letter back from her in response. Of the many comments I have received from people whose lives I have been privileged to touch, none has been more poignant to me than this one from Lilly, for it is the legacy we leave to those closest to us that matters most. Here is an excerpt from Lilly's letter:

When I grow up and get to you and Nonna's age I want to be just like you guys. I want to travel, have the perfect family, be with the one I love all the time, and be retired. And it's not just me, all the girl cousins would just talk and talk about how we wanted to be just like you and Nonna. You guys have the perfect life and you started with nothing but each other. I think that's pretty amazing! That's why you are one of my biggest role models.

Every individual will have their own reasons for personal development, but there are also some universal *whys*. There are also tools to focus and strengthen your *why*. This is important because real change doesn't come cheaply. It takes a strong *why* to be willing to pay the price for change and the success that follows. Lilly wants the best life has to offer, and with every fiber of my being, I want her to have it. My *why* is all the Lillys of this world.

1

HAPPINESS

THE PURPOSE OF LIFE IS TO BE HAPPY

"Indeed, man wishes to be happy even when
he lives as to make happiness impossible."

~ St. Augustine ~

Since the beginning of recorded time, scores of philosophers, mystics, poets, and academics have contemplated the purpose of mankind. They ask, "What is the purpose of life? Does mankind have a universal desire?" Generally, these thinkers come to the same conclusion Aristotle reached when he declared, "Happiness is the meaning and the purpose of life, the whole aim and end of human existence." One of the great sages of our era, the Dalai Lama, put it succinctly: "I believe that the very purpose of life is to be happy." If you are a parent, you have come to the same conclusion as the great thinkers, for you have undoubtedly said, at some point, "All I want for my children is for them to be happy." Why would we choose happiness for our children if we didn't think it was the greatest gift life has to offer and what we most want for ourselves? *The purpose of life is to be happy,* and happiness is the universal desire of mankind.

When we make poor decisions, we make them based on what we think will make us happiest. We know in the long run, it won't really make us happy to sit on the sofa, eat a quart of ice cream, and binge-watch Netflix. Intellectually, we know we will most likely feel sick from the ice cream and be disappointed in the wasted time. In the emotion of the moment when we make such a decision, we hope it will somehow be different this time, even if past experience has proven otherwise. While it provided some brief pleasure that could be misconstrued as happiness, it is not happiness itself.

Our good decisions are also based on what will make us happy. For example, we may still be tempted to eat a quart of ice cream and binge-watch Netflix, but we know from experience we will be happier if we eat a healthy dinner and do something productive. When we face a chore we would rather not do, like cleaning the kitchen or mowing the lawn, we don't complete the chore because the actual cleaning and mowing make us happy (although it might). We do it because we know a clean kitchen feels better, and the mowed lawn will give us a sense of satisfaction in a job completed. The end result is that we are happier than if we leave it undone. We make choices, big and small, day in and day out, for the sake of happiness because...

The purpose of life is to be happy

THE KEY TO HAPPINESS

"I am incapable of conceiving infinity, and yet I do not accept finity. I want this adventure that is the context of my life to go on without end."

~ Simone de Beauvoir ~

It is easy to believe everyone wants to be happy, or happier, but what makes people happy? Is there a different answer for each person, or is there a universal answer? I asked this question while speaking at a reception for fifty women who were being recognized for their contribution to business by the WCA (Women and Children's Alliance). The audience was 250 successful, educated, and accomplished people. After discussing happiness as the purpose of our existence, to which they readily agreed, I asked them, "What is the key to happiness?" A few hesitatingly offered suggestions like "service," or "love," but their suggestions sounded more like questions than answers. Just as the universal desire of mankind is to be happy, there is a universal answer to what makes people happy. I have addressed this topic with other groups with the same results. Once I reveal that *personal progression toward an infinite potential is the key to happiness*, heads nod in agreement. Some nod because they already knew this to be true on some level. Others nod because if there is a universal answer to what makes people happy, then this is the only one that makes sense.[1]

Ralph Waldo Emerson visited the sequoias and marveled, "It's a wonder that we can see these trees and not wonder more." I have often stood at the base of those trees, looked up, and marveled myself. As wonderful as those redwood trees are, I am more in awe of humans, both as they are and what they are capable of. Did you know that even though the redwood is the tallest and most majestic of trees, its coniferous cone is very small—only about an inch long? Like the redwood cone, we, too, are small and unimpressive in many ways, but we have within us the power to be majestic. We each have unimaginable, unlimited, infinite potential!

In the Hebrew Torah, the psalmist sings, "Thou has made him (man) a little lower than God and crowned him with glory and honor," or at least the possibility of glory and honor. Abraham Maslow expressed the contradiction between our "nothingness" and our infinite possibility when he said, "We are simultaneously worms and gods." Every time we become a little better and move a little closer to that divine, infinite, marvelous potential, we are a little happier because *personal progression toward an infinite potential is the key to happiness.*

---

[1] View this discussion online at https://bit.ly/2JaUefJ

The idea that there was a correlation between personal growth and happiness was in the back of my mind for years. It was almost certainly introduced to me by some of the great thinkers whose works I had read, but I can't tell you who because I don't remember. I do remember when it became a crystal clear truth to me.

My husband, Ken, and I enjoy road trips, and we like listening to motivational or inspirational material while we drive. We will frequently turn the program off in order to talk about the ideas we just heard. It makes for inspiring conversation and the sharing of ideas. Sometimes we get excited about these ideas, and many of them have contributed to our success in various enterprises as well as relationships. In this particular case, we were listening to an audiobook called *Ultimate Goals* by Brian Tracy, on our way home from Las Vegas. Even though we are fans of Brian Tracy, we were struggling to stay interested in this particular book until he began talking about *daily written goals*. We were both intrigued and began the practice as soon as we arrived home.[2]

We practiced daily written goals exactly as Brian Tracy explained it, and in just a few weeks, I was amazed at the progress I was making with a particular habit that had plagued me for years. I am embarrassed to admit it, but the habit was *gossip*. I would set goals, pray for help, and distance myself from some friends in an effort to smash this bad habit. I would make some progress for a while and then backslide. I literally worked on this for years! You cannot imagine how many times I left a conversation frustrated and ashamed of myself because of a critical remark I made about another person. After a couple of weeks of daily written goals—or daily written affirmations, as we call them now—I had almost completely eradicated this habit. I was also making good progress in some other areas. I was energized and excited about life. This was fifteen years ago, but I still distinctly remember walking toward a restaurant to meet my sisters for lunch and feeling like I was walking on air! I had an elevated feeling of well-being, and I absolutely knew it was due to the progress I was making. I had only taken baby steps toward my

---

[2] You'll learn more about daily written goals in Chapter 11.

potential, but the possibilities of what else I might become seemed infinite. I was so happy!

If you are doubtful that *personal progression toward an infinite potential is the key to happiness*, I suggest you try this experiment. Do something that challenges you, something hard. Hike a steep hill, take a small gift to someone you don't particularly like, make that call you have been dreading, or apologize to someone you have offended, especially if you believe you were justified. Gather up all your courage and do it, then see what your happiness level feels like. You will be proud of yourself! And because you like yourself more, your self-esteem will increase. You will stretch, you will grow, and you will be better than you were. You will be happier because...

Personal progression toward an infinite potential is the key to happiness

DESTINED FOR GREATNESS

"Nothing great has ever been achieved except by those who dared believe that something inside them was superior to circumstances."

~ Bruce Barton ~

Personal progression toward an infinite potential is the key to happiness, and it is a simple concept, but it isn't necessarily an easy one to practice. If you asked any room full of ambitious college students to raise their hand if they would like to achieve a life that includes a romantic and sexy marriage, a satisfying spiritual life, close family relationships, good friends, financial independence, career success, a strong intellect, being physically fit, and the ability to make the world a better place, every hand would go up, right? Yet it is estimated only 3–5% of people actually achieve that kind of success in life, and it isn't because of circumstances or opportunities. People from every background, race, financial circumstance, and physical ability have been successful.

Humans are like seed-filled cones of the redwoods. Most crumble in the ground without reaching their grand potential. They die with their songs unsung, their dreams still inside them, and much of their glorious potential wasted. Unlike redwood cones, which have no choice but to accept their fate, we have the power to change our conditions. We can decide what we want to become. The possibilities are infinitely fabulous, and yet so many settle for so little.

My parents divorced when I was seven, and my mother moved us to a little town in Utah. This was in 1962, when people looked down on divorced women. To make matters worse, my mother was not well-equipped to be raising four little girls on her own. She had not graduated from high school, and she had little money. Within a year, she married a local man who was a stereotypical abusive alcoholic. We were definitely the poor white trash of Brigham City. No one was mean to me that I can recall, and occasionally we were recipients of exceptional kindness from people in the community, such as one lady who sewed clothes for us. But we were also not embraced, either.

I was only eight and nine years old, but I was a little feral. I would wander downtown alone and go to the movies, which consisted of two full-length movies plus cartoons in those days. I would walk to the community swimming pool and spend hours jumping off the high dive. I couldn't swim, so I would dog paddle to the side of the pool. Another favorite pastime was browsing the local drugstore, and sometimes I would steal small things I had no use for. In spite of my circumstances, and even at that young age, I felt that I was someone special. I believed I was *destined for greatness*. I just needed to find the way to that nebulous something waiting out there for me. How I came to feel I was especially singled out for great things I do not know, and how I managed to hold on to that feeling during a childhood that could have destroyed me is baffling. I have known many people over the years, including my children, who marvel that I am not apparently scarred by my childhood. I find myself surprised at their surprise because I never thought my circumstances were problematic. I knew I was someone special, and I was waiting for the great things destiny had in store for me. I don't know where this attitude came from, but I was lucky to have it. Fortunately, you do not need luck. You can simply *decide* you are worthy of success and then get out there and do great things.

Things might have gotten worse for my family and me, but a miracle happened. When I was ten years old, my parents divorced their current spouses and reunited. Life was better. We moved to a small ranch in southeast Idaho, where I rode horses and excelled at debate. I had friends, dated, and had the usual teenage social life, but I still spent a lot of time alone. I was a thinker and a reader, and I wanted to know the secret to a successful life. The counselor at my high school once told me it was normal for teens to want to fit in and then asked why I didn't feel that way. The very question caused me a slight sense of panic. The world had big plans for me, and how could I be classified as special if I blended in?

How was I going to achieve that special, unique life? I had no idea! I didn't even know what it would look like, but I was always looking for some wise little tidbit that might be the key to what I longed for. When I was fifteen, I read the book *I'm Okay – You're Okay* by Thomas Anthony Harris. It was popular at the time, and the first thing I ever read in the personal development genre. I also read parts of the New Testament Gospels repeatedly, and like many angst-ridden teens, I read *The Prophet* by Kahlil Gibran. I searched out and collected pithy one-liners about living at a higher level, such as "Where your treasure is, there will your heart be also," and I collected quotes that felt like truths to me.

It may sound like I was a wise child, but I was also immature in a lot of ways. I graduated at age seventeen, and because my family was once again falling apart, I was on my own from that point—too immature to be without the structure of a family, and I was itching for trouble. I began drinking and quickly developed an alcohol problem. I frequently paid bills late or not at all, and I went back to shoplifting when I ran out of money. If I couldn't afford to go where I wanted, I hitchhiked. I was living in the moment and only interested in having fun. I was a wild child without discipline or direction.

THE ROAD TO CHANGE

"We do not usually make significant and lasting changes in quantum leaps. All permanent change is progressive over a long period of time. This type of change requires patience and discipline. It is only this type of change that is worthwhile and enduring."

~ Brian Tracy ~

The incongruity between the person I was and the person I am now is so striking that I frequently hear comments about it. One of my longtime friends said he knows of no one who has come as far in life as my husband and me. He said this not so much because of where we are, but because of where we were when we started.

Ken was from California, just north of San Francisco, a hub of drug culture. We both graduated from high school in 1973, which was at the end of the Vietnam War. The hippie movement was still in full swing, drugs were a way of life, and crazy concerts were an attraction since Woodstock. We were a new generation who said we wanted something different than the old one, but mostly we just wanted to party. Ken and I had both been living this way when we met in 1976. I had a baby the year before, in 1975. Ken loved her as much as I did, and it was our love for her and our concern for her welfare that caused us to forsake our current lifestyle and *join the establishment* by getting married.

We loved our little family, but we had nothing! We had partied away the time and resources we might have put into education or financial stability. Nevertheless, and against the odds, I was once again back to expecting big things in my life. Fortunately, Ken felt the same way. We believed we were superior to our circumstances and just needed to find a way to the success we knew was possible. Eventually, we did find success beyond our wildest dreams. It often works that way, but it took some time and an education they don't teach at a university.

Ken worked for low wages, and I did childcare in our home so I could be with our children. We struggled to pay our bills and put food on the table. We worked hard and stayed hopeful that things would change, but it was discouraging. We attempted a few ventures, but they failed. I distinctly remember a day when our circumstances brought us to our knees. Ken had been working days at his job and building picnic tables with a friend to sell for extra money in the evenings. His days were long. We had four children, and I was still doing childcare, so my days were long as well. The stress of the situation caused an argument, which was rare for us. Afterward, we sat on the bed side by side and shed tears of despair. I wondered what would become of us and what happens to people like us if we don't make it. Would the earth just open and swallow us up?

Over the next ten years, we were able to move our family into increasingly nicer homes and better lifestyles. Within fifteen years of that experience, we were independently wealthy. Our marriage is loving, warm, companionable, and romantic. Our family is thriving. We are physically fit. We have traveled the world. We have had marvelous opportunities to influence the lives of others. I live in a downtown condo with my fabulous husband, and from our balcony, we have a nice view of the city we love. We marvel at the unique and beautiful life we have. It took time, but gradually we became the people that Lilly admires. Our life is not perfect, but it is fabulous, and by all measures, we are successful.

Why did we achieve these things when most do not? We had three things going for us: We loved each other completely; we adored our little family; and we trusted God. However, a lot of young couples have those things but still live and die poor. We had observed this and were not interested in that plan and knew there had to be more to it.

About two years after we were married, I saw a book at my mother's house called *See You at the Top* by Zig Ziglar. I picked it up, took it home, and read it. Then Ken read it. We learned a few things about success. We continued to read a book here and listen to an audio programs there. In spite of a very busy life, we were pretty good at applying the principles. We were working hard, but time was precious, so progress was slow, but we were changing our thinking, increasing our discipline, and developing new habits.

One of the first things I did was to make myself a small chart. I now call this a tracking sheet, and in "Part III: How," I will go into more detail. My original tracking sheet was an index card containing three daily habits I wanted to acquire. Every day, I would check the items off as I completed them. I taped the card on a cabinet in my kitchen, where friends and extended family members could see it. There was no way I wanted anyone to see that I missed something, so my pride became my accountability partner. I doubt anyone ever noticed my little chart, but that tracking sheet motivated me and helped me develop lifelong habits. I felt then, and still feel today, driven to be the best I can be in every area of life. Because of this drive, I continue to track daily, weekly, and monthly goals. I have added items to my tracking sheet over the years. Some of those first items are now such deeply ingrained habits that tracking them is unnecessary. This practice helped me develop lifelong, life-changing habits.

Real progress is not swift. I am always suspicious of quick, sweeping changes anywhere, but especially in the lives of people. Significant change comes with the consistent application of correct principles and practices over an extended period of time. That's the way it was for us. We had already been making some significant changes in our lives when we sat on the edge of the bed in that moment of despair, and it wasn't the last discouraging episode of our lives. The discouraging moments are part of the process. It is in those discouraging moments that people quit. I learned to think of those moments as a test. Success is on the other side of discouragement if we can just hold on.

Most high achievers, from Aristotle (who had Plato) to modern philosophers, athletes, businessmen, and great musicians, have used mentors or coaches to reach their full potential. We had a few personal mentors, but most were authors and lecturers. Successful people spend an inordinate amount of their income on coaching, mentoring, and other personal development programs. We continually read books and listened to audioprograms. Some were better than others. Earl Nightingale's *The Strangest Secret* had a major impact. Ken always recommends the audiobook to people he mentors. We also listened to all of Wayne Dyer's audioprograms. We then scraped up the money to attend seminars by some of these great motivators and teachers such as Zig Ziglar, Brian Tracy, Hyrum Smith, and Wayne Dyer. A series of experiential, personal development workshops we attended deepened and refined our understanding of principles of success and our infinite potential for progression. In 2015, I attended Darren Hardy's High-Performance Forum. We had been hit hard by the recession, and money was still tight. In my journal, I wrote, "This event cost $13,000 plus flight, hotel, and ground transportation. It is a lot of money and a great opportunity for me. I intend to get all I can out of this experience." I did, and it was worth every cent.

WHAT ABOUT BEING CONTENT?

"I am content with who I am, and who I am
is someone who is always progressing."

~ Chad Powell ~

It may appear, at first, that contentment and the drive for progression cannot coexist in the same individual, but like many of life's ironies, they are not only compatible but are necessary to one another. The real enemy of contentment is stagnation. It is easy to confuse contentment with complacency. Complacency is the enemy of progress. A static life breeds discontent and restlessness, not contentment or happiness.

For nine years, I worked with ninth-graders from the local junior high school. Every year I would ask the current class if they loved being in ninth grade. I already knew they did. They were freshmen, the BMOC (big man on campus), and experiencing more freedom as well as opportunities than ever before. After letting them explain how wonderful ninth grade was, I would ask who wanted to be a ninth-grader again next year. No one did. The thought was revolting. It was far more important to these kids to progress than it was to stay at the school they loved. Should we be content with what we have and who we are? The answer is a resounding YES! We must be content with *where* we are and *who* we are before we can change.

When asked how he was, Zig Ziglar always responded, "Outstanding! But I am improving." While it is important to know you are fine the way you are, it is also important to know you are not intended to stay as you are. You were not put on this earth to be *fine;* you were put on this earth to be *better.* To do that, you will need to be content with who you are *and* continuously improving. To be continuously improving is to be happy. I said earlier that personal progression toward an infinite potential is the key to happiness, and it is, but there is one more part of the equation. The full formula for happiness looks like this:

Contentment + Progress = Happiness

Contentment with yourself is necessary for change because we absolutely need a strong self-image to know we are capable and deserving of the best life has to offer. I believed this about myself against all odds. I do not know why, but I did. After giving up the wild lifestyle of "drugs, sex, and rock and roll," I began considering spiritual things more seriously. As I came to know God better, I realized God didn't love me more than other people, as I had thought. Like any excellent parent, He loves all of His children equally. I then thought, *I guess I am not particularly special after all.* A few more years of understanding brought me full circle. I realized how God loving all His children doesn't make me less special. The advantage I had was that I knew I was destined for great things. I felt it deeply enough that I would work for it. You are also destined for greatness, infinitely capable, and deserving. It is critical that you believe in your own potential for greatness.

I want you to want more, and to believe you can have it. I want you to see the possibilities and learn how to achieve your dreams. It isn't an easy journey or a quick fix, but it is a glorious adventure. You are your own masterpiece. The happiness that comes in moving toward your *infinite* potential is not about *arriving* at that potential. Because your possibilities are *infinite,* you can never *arrive.* Not in this life. It is your *journey* that creates your *happiness.* Because *happiness* is in the *journey,* a happier life begins with the first forward step you take. Happiness increases with every forward step.

2

FIRST THINGS FIRST

TEACHERS TEACH SOMEONE

"I cannot be a teacher without exposing who I am."

~ Paulo Freire ~

For nearly thirty years, I have been speaking to audiences of all sizes, and I have been coaching as well as mentoring for over a decade. It's in my heart to do these things because I am a *teacher*, not by training but by an inner passion. Speaking, workshops, coaching, writing…these are simply platforms for teaching.

The progression of becoming a teacher:

1. Learn something valuable.
2. Practice it until you become successful.
3. Teach it to others.

There were undoubtedly times in your life when you followed this formula naturally. Parenting is an obvious example. You teach your children the basic skills of life, from walking to driving a car. You learned them yourself, practiced them for years, and then taught

16

your children. In your profession, you have learned your craft and almost certainly at some point have mentored a newer employee. You were their mentor because you learned the skills and became proficient enough to model them effectively.

There are a lot of people in this world who want to teach you something, sell you their ideas, or sell you someone else's ideas, but have skipped step two—*practice it until you become successful.*

I learned the hard way that the minute a teacher makes teaching about themselves, about looking smart or clever or teaching anything for the purpose of getting invited to speak again, or solely to promote their business, they have lost the day.

A real teacher teaches with only the success and well-being of the student in mind. Samuel Natale was right when he said, "Teachers teach someone something, in that order." The topic is less important than the student. A good math teacher doesn't teach math to students; he teaches students math and does it without consideration of self. To teach someone something, in that order, is the only way to truly influence a life as a teacher.

When one teaches, two learn. On occasion, I have had a new insight into a concept I was teaching at the very moment I was teaching it. It is a wonderful, enlightening experience, but it doesn't happen unless I am very prepared. When a coach or teacher of any kind gives their best effort with the only thought of blessing the student, they too are blessed with a few steps toward their own potential. To teach a *quart* of knowledge effectively, the teacher must have a *gallon* of information and understanding. Teaching a *quart* of information when you only have a quart is to not have the depth to be credible or enlightening. To teach a *quart,* when you only have a *pint* of knowledge and experience, is absurd, even though there are those who do it and appear to have a following.

The concepts and practices I teach have come through personal learning and many years of refining what I have learned through practice. My goal is to facilitate your progress, and thereby your happiness. I will not write anything on these pages I do not know to be true by my own experience. I have proved the principles and practices laid out and found success. This is the book I wish I had when I was younger. If I assist you in running further and flying higher, that will be the measure of my success.

There is no status quo in the universe—everyone and everything is thriving or dying, like those redwood cones molding on the ground. There are some people who refuse to thrive. For example, Ken was asked to mentor a man in dire need of changing his circumstances. However, instead of talking about what he might do to improve his situation, this man talked about the host of people he blames for his problems, some of them long dead. I have had coaching clients begin each session, if I let them, doing what I call "looping." They rehearse the people and situations that are, in their minds, holding them back. I gently remind them how we have already covered that territory and have work to do. If I cannot get them past this habit, I will terminate our agreement because they aren't interested in changing; they just want to blame or complain.

These six things are required before anyone can make large strides forward in their own personal development and enjoy the happiness that is the companion to progress:

1. Know change is possible.
2. Be accountable for current circumstances.
3. Have a desire to change.
4. Educate about change.
5. Apply that knowledge.
6. Stay committed.

KNOW CHANGE IS POSSIBLE

"Argue for your limitations, and sure enough, they're yours."

~ Richard Bach ~

Full-grown elephants are generally tethered by a small rope tied around their right rear leg. They could easily break the rope, yet they stay tied to the spot regardless of their desire to move about freely. When they are very young, they are tied to immovable stakes by chains. They struggle for a period of three or four weeks to free themselves and then give up. They have now been conditioned to believe they cannot move when their right rear leg is tied. The adult elephant doesn't try to leave because it doesn't know it can break the rope!

Many people have been conditioned to believe what they want is unattainable. This self-limiting belief impedes their efforts to progress and thereby stunts their opportunity for increased happiness.

In 2009, I opened a boutique fitness business called *FitMania*. We had three locations and hundreds of clients over the nine years I spent running the business. I would frequently have clients, or potential clients, in my office who desperately wanted to be lean and strong but could not believe it was possible for them. There were plenty of people in our program who started in similar situations and were achieving their goals. That should have been evidence enough that it was possible, but even after seeing the results others were getting, many people did not believe they were capable of achieving their dreams. They seemed to think the attainment of fitness was for other people. They sincerely believed they were not capable or, sadly, did not deserve the body they wanted.

What have you been conditioned to believe about your body that holds you back?

What have you been conditioned to believe about your earning potential that holds you back?

What have you been conditioned to believe about money that holds you back?

What are you conditioned to believe about relationships that hold you back?

What have you been conditioned to believe about your intellect that holds you back?

What have you been conditioned to believe about yourself that holds you back?

Every one of us can do more and be more than we think we can. Don't be held back by false beliefs about yourself.

BE ACCOUNTABLE

"If it's never our fault, we can't take responsibility for it. If we can't take responsibility for it, we'll always be its victim."

~ Richard Bach ~

One of the key elements to effective change is accountability. You must know that you are where you are because of the decisions you have made, at least in part. You can't feel like a victim of your circumstances and move forward at the same time. Once you understand that it is the choices you have made that have landed you where you are, you can see that it is your choices that will get you out.

A victim mentality is a belief that the past is more powerful than the present. It is also the belief that other people and what they did to you are responsible for your pain and for who you have become. If events and other people have caused your current circumstances, you are powerless. All you can do is wait for events and people to make things better.

Accountability is the opposite of a victim mentality. When you realize you choose your direction, the people you allow in your life, and the way you think about things, you will feel empowered. Once you know that there are plenty of things within your control, it's time to go to work.

Our circumstances are rarely free of some influence from the decisions of others, as well as biological, social, educational, and cultural influences. Teryl Givens wrote, "Secondhand smoke of a thousand types complicates and compromises the degree of freedom and accountability behind every human choice."

It is also true that every situation has the opportunity for accountability. Consider this example: *You* decide to drive to the grocery store. *You* decide to take a particular route at a particular time. *You* have a lot on your mind, so this ride seems the perfect time to think. As you go through an intersection, someone runs a red light and crashes into the passenger side of your car. Is it your fault? Of course not. Do you have any accountability? Yes. *You* chose to go to the store. *You* chose when to go. *You* chose the route. *You* were also a little preoccupied and perhaps not watching closely enough. None of those things were wrong. You did nothing wrong, and you had no way of knowing this accident would happen. However, you made decisions that put you in that place at that time. Now, there are a couple more decisions to be made. How will *you* respond to this situation? How will *you* treat the offender? Most importantly, will *you* choose to be a victim? Will you tell your friends how you cannot believe this guy ran that light and smacked right into you? Or will you say, "Had I been paying a little more attention, I might have saved both the driver and me a lot of grief." This is not being at fault—it is being accountable. It is not the events in our lives that determine who we become; it is how we process those events. It takes great maturity to be accountable, but it can be very empowering. It can also bring peace to the situation and to those involved.

You may have read *Man's Search for Meaning,* where Viktor Frankl tells of men in the concentration camps in Germany who would give away their last crust of bread. Frankl wrote, "Between stimulus and response there is a space. In that space is our power to choose our response. In our response lies our growth and our freedom." Not many of those men gave away their precious food. Most fought for every crumb, but enough men shared to prove that even when every option seems to be taken away, we can still choose.

There is an upside to having a victim mentality. The benefit of being a victim may include the satisfaction of being right, getting attention, validation for your suffering from well-meaning people, and having a built-in excuse for not taking control of your own life. Yes, it has a payoff, and it is addictive, but it is shallow compensation for all that you lose.

Portia Nelson does a beautiful job of describing the process from victimhood to accountability in her brief poem "There's a hole in my sidewalk."

Chapter 1
I walk down the street.
There is a deep hole in the sidewalk.
I fall in.
I am lost...I am helpless.
It isn't my fault.
It takes forever to find a way out.

Chapter 2
I walk down the street.
There is a deep hole in the sidewalk.
I pretend that I don't see it.
I fall in again.
I can't believe I am in this same place.
But it isn't my fault.
It still takes a long time to get out.

Chapter 3
I walk down the same street.
There is a deep hole in the sidewalk.
I see it is there.
I still fall in...it's a habit.
My eyes are open.
I know where I am.
It is *my* fault.
I get out immediately.

Chapter 4
I walk down the same street.
There is a deep hole in the sidewalk.
I walk around it.

Chapter 5
I walk down another street.

While my parents were divorced, things happened that shouldn't happen to a child. When they were together, we moved constantly. My dad was a dreamer and always looking for the next big thing, so by the time I started junior high, I had lived in fifteen different houses and attended nine different grade schools. Maybe it fit me, and it definitely shaped me, but I have no resentments about my childhood. I actually liked it. It gave me a lot of autonomy to think my own thoughts and live my own way. There were plenty of downsides, of course, but I like myself, and if you like yourself, you have to embrace everything that has ever happened to you. Every experience molds us in some way. If you like yourself, embrace it all. If you do not, then go to work and become someone you can be proud of.

HAVE A DESIRE TO CHANGE

"There is one quality which one must possess to win, and that is definiteness of purpose, the knowledge of what one wants, and a burning desire to possess it."

~ Napoleon Hill ~

There once was a caterpillar who did not know what she wanted to do with her life. She wandered aimlessly until she saw another caterpillar hanging upside down on a branch, caught in some hairy substance. She said, "You seem to be in some trouble. Can I help you?"

"No," said the hanging caterpillar. "I have to do this to become a butterfly."

The crawling caterpillar asked, "Butterfly? What is a butterfly?"

The hanging caterpillar replied, "It's what you are meant to be. It flies with beautiful wings and joins the earth to heaven. It drinks

23

only nectar from flowers and carries seeds of love from one flower to another. Without butterflies, the world would soon have few flowers."

The crawling caterpillar exclaimed, "It can't be true! How can I believe there's a butterfly inside me when all I see is a fuzzy worm? How does one become a butterfly?"

The hanging caterpillar answered, "You must want to be a butterfly so much that you are willing to give up being a caterpillar."

Every goal is comprised of 80% intention and 20% mechanics. If your intention is clear, then you will find a way to reach your goal. Finding the way might even change from feeling impossible to being fun.

The junior high kids I worked with were high achievers. They were good students who were involved in sports, music, and leadership activities. At one point, I challenged them to commit to a daily reading habit. There was much conversation about how they wanted to take this challenge, but they didn't think they had the time. We walked to the indoor basketball court, and I had all twenty of them line up on one side. I asked each of them to cross the floor one at a time. They could walk, run, skip, etc., but no two people could cross using the same method. They initially thought it was impossible to come up with enough different ways to cross, and those who would be last didn't think they had a chance. One crawled, one walked sideways, one skipped, and soon they had all crossed the gym.

I then asked them to cross back with the stipulation that they couldn't use any of the previous methods. Again they groaned and said it wasn't possible, but eventually, they danced, somersaulted, did jumping jacks, and everyone was across the floor again. We did it a third time, and they *still* found new ways to cross. The more creative they became, the more we laughed. It was so fun that they wanted to cross again. They now understood that if they truly desired to do something, they could find a way. They accepted the daily challenge I gave them, and for the rest of the school year, those kids maintained that habit. I frequently had parents and other teachers ask me how I managed to get them to do it. It honestly never occurred to me that they wouldn't, or couldn't, or that it was too much to ask. My job, as the teacher, was to make them see the possibility and to build their desire. Those kids are all adults now. I run into one occasionally who will report that they still have their daily habit.

Someone may come along and build a desire in you, but don't wait around for that. You do not have time, and what if no one ever does? Besides, all another person can do is to add fuel to a desire that already exists within you.

Even after marrying a marvelous man and building a beautiful life together, there were moments when I had to say to myself, "There is no one but me." No one but me to carry this particular burden. No one but me to motivate me to do what needs to be done! In our journey, there will be many people who lend support in many ways. If you are looking around for enough desire to change your world, I would suggest you say to yourself, "There is no one but me."

Knowing there is no one but you can strengthen your desire to change. I learned this in 1975 when I was nineteen, single, and pregnant. I had intended to give my baby up for adoption. I had filled out the paperwork and was seeing a required counselor. I had never wanted children and certainly not in these circumstances. At that point, I did not have a maternal bone in my entire body! One day, I had a remarkable experience—an epiphany, if you will—and I knew I needed to keep my baby. Throughout the entire pregnancy, I never experienced a single maternal instinct or desire to be a mother. But the moment they laid that baby girl in my arms, my whole world changed! I didn't know it was possible to love anyone like I loved that baby. I was still nineteen years old with a child to care for. The father was not available, and my family was a mess, again. My parents loved me but couldn't offer much emotional or financial support. I managed okay sometimes, and sometimes I didn't. There were a few desperate moments when I reached out for help, but there was no one there. I still remember the moment I said to myself, "There is no one but me." I quit feeling sorry for myself and just took care of things the best I could. Once I took control of my own destiny, my desire to change was fortified.

EDUCATE YOURSELF ABOUT CHANGE

"Education is not the filling of a pail, but the lighting of a fire."
~ William Butler Yeats ~

Belief in yourself is both powerful and necessary, but you wouldn't expect a surgeon to operate on you with only a desire and knowing it is possible. We expect our surgeon to be educated on the procedure and to have obtained the necessary practice. Whatever our field of endeavor, we understand the need for education and experience before we can be successful. This is your life! If you want to be successful in it, you will need an education. You will need a certain kind of expertise to become who you want to be and to gain the success you want. This expertise requires skills, practice, and time.

This education must be sought out. You will need to read, or listen to, many books. You will attend seminars, as well as seek out coaches and mentors. You will watch the habits of the successful people you admire. You will need to learn effective goal-setting techniques and discover other tools for success, such as the value of a mission statement or governing values, which are taught in Chapter Three. You will also require effective methods for tracking and systems for habit building, which are taught in Chapter Eleven.

With all my heart, I hope the things I write here influence your life in wonderful ways. However, regardless of how effectively I write or how valuable my information (and my information is quite valuable), it will not be enough. As the pursuit of excellence becomes a way of life, it will, by necessity, be accompanied by the pursuit of knowledge. In the pursuit of excellence, we will never see a time when we will not need to be taught.

In your pursuit of excellence, be careful from whom you take advice. If someone would teach you something, it is fair to ask them how they know that thing to be true. If they are an author or lecturer, research them. Find out if they have the kind of success in their own lives you desire to have in yours.

When I signed up for the seminar with Darren Hardy, I did it with confidence because I had read Darren's books, subscribed to *Success* magazine, of which he was the editor, and most importantly, I knew he had been successful himself. I knew he was teaching from his own experience. I learned more at that seminar than I could ever apply. I want to learn from the man or woman who has gone out into the world, made something happen, and now has, through their own experience, some things to teach the rest of us.

There is a very popular motivational speaker and writer who I should like. He teaches things I believe to be true, but I cannot take him seriously. His only career has been telling other people how to live, and yet his personal life has not been stellar, and his language is often profane. He is a showman, and no matter how good his advice or great his popularity, I cannot respect him enough to learn from him.

One young man, who I knew quite well, contacted me immediately after graduating from college. He wanted to meet with me. He had some ideas on how to run my business and thought I should hire him as a consultant, even though he was fresh out of college and had never run a business. Ken and I are serial entrepreneurs with thirty-five years of experience. I also had access to some brilliantly successful people who mentored or advised me. I respectfully suggested this young man run a business first and get some experience. I have no doubt he will one day be wonderfully successful, but I could not afford to take advice from someone without real experience, regardless of how much I liked him.

I also recall a young woman who graduated from college. When Ken asked her what her plans were, she wasn't sure but thought she might be a life coach. He politely suggested she live a little first. She smiled and agreed.

Obviously, life experience is not the only way we become knowledgeable. Growing older does not necessarily mean we are growing wiser. My dad had some very enlightened views of the world when I was a teenager, and those views often became my views. However, education must be constantly used, renewed, and added to. My dad didn't do that. I was disappointed when, in his later years, he became less enlightened, less educated, and less tolerant.

There are many coaching programs out there that teach people how to coach. You read their book or take their course, and they certify you to coach. Some are pretty good, but most are just businesses. Before I choose a coach, I want to know they are on higher ground than I am. I ask the following questions:

Have they been successful in managing their health?
Have they been successful in managing their finances?
Are their relationships successful?

A man might say, "I have been married three times, so I know a lot about marriage." No, he knows a lot about divorce. The person who knows a lot about marriage is the one who has been happily married for a very long time. Someone might declare they are an expert in finance because they have advanced degrees in finance. Unless they have amassed their own fortune, then what they know is how to get degrees in finance. Taking advice from well-meaning but unsuccessful people won't ruin you, but it might leave you confused and waste your precious time.

You can learn valuable lessons from people who have expertise in one particular area and are successful in that one thing. However, the mentors who have had the greatest impact on me are the ones who are successful in every important aspect of life. Remember, the progression of becoming a teacher is to learn something valuable, practice it until you are successful (which will deepen and refine the concept), and then teach it to others. This will deepen and refine the concept even further. I know that by the time this book is printed, I will have learned something new about the very principles I am teaching here, and I will wish I had known that thing in time to include it. That is the way of continuing education.

APPLY WHAT YOU LEARN

*"In theory, there is no difference between theory and practice.
But in practice, there is."*

~ Jan L. A. van de Snepscheut ~

When our daughter, Merry, was a toddler, I spent time with a friend who also had a child. We enjoyed long bike rides together while the kids napped in their attached seats behind us. We talked about books and shared ideas as we peddled. On more than one occasion, we discussed a book we both liked. I asked her what she was going to do with what she had learned. Her response was usually, "Nothing." I was repeatedly dumbfounded. Why did she read the books? Our friendship didn't last very long. Not only was she not moving forward, but she also became increasingly cynical about life.

A lot of people read personal development books and attend motivational events, but still don't find success. The secret is not just obtaining the information and the motivation. That is fairly easy. Major life events can be a wake-up call, but most people don't stay awake long enough to change. The secret is in the *consistent* application of what you learn through intentional learning or by life's lessons. It is what you do every day, day after day, that makes you equal to the success you desire. This work is about becoming a person who is attaining their infinite potential. There are no shortcuts.

STAY COMMITTED

"It is determination and commitment to an unrelenting pursuit of your goal that will enable you to attain the success you seek."

~ Mario Andretti ~

What you think about is vital to your success. A single negative thought can derail you, while a powerful positive thought can be a second wind, giving you new energy to charge forward. If you change a thought that might make you quit into one that keeps you going, and you do it often enough, it will mean the difference between a mediocre life and a successful one.

There are a number of power phrases I use in my life to stay motivated when things are tough. The statement I choose is the one I need at that moment. I repeat it over and over as long as necessary. To keep our clients motivated at FitMania, I filled the walls of our studio with some of those phrases. Here are my favorites:

What you think about expands

When I drive from Boise to Utah, I pass some government-sponsored signs warning DROWSY DRIVERS CAUSE CRASHES. As soon as I see the word drowsy, I immediately feel sleepy. The creator of those signs missed a universal principle Earl Nightingale called *The Strangest Secret*. It is a principle that weaves its way through most religions and through all modern personal development philosophies. It is the principle that *we are what we think about.*

When I trained fitness classes, I was fond of saying, "Remember, *The Little Engine That Could* is a true story!" Of course, the story is not technically true, but it is a true principle. If you think tired thoughts during a workout, you slow down. If you think strong, *I can* thoughts, you speed up and feel energized. If you focus on points of pain, you will feel fragile, but if you focus on how healthy your body is, you will feel strong, and pain will take a back seat. We are what we think about, or as Wayne Dyer put it, "What you think about expands."

You can always do more than you think you can

Not long after our tearful night of despair, Ken quit his job, and we started a construction supply business. Within a few years, the business was flourishing, and so were we. But we were busy! We now had six children and a calendar full of baseball games, track meets, cross-country meets, wrestling meets, dance lessons, dance performances, choir performances, piano recitals, and drama performances. We also had coaching, carpools, dance costumes, and sports equipment to organize. We were involved in our community and had heavy church responsibilities as well. I would think through my day in the morning while I was running, walking, or riding my bike. To fight the feeling of being overwhelmed by my responsibilities, I would repeat to myself, "I can always do more than I think I can." And I could. I proved it over and over.

Obviously, you cannot keep cramming more into the day, but I had a certain number of things that had to be done. I could choose to have a positive attitude and enjoy the day, or I could choose to feel stressed. Believe me, I tried it both ways. If I could get my *Little Engine That Could* attitude in place before the day was too far underway, my day went much better. *You can do more when you are happy.*

Another trick to doing more than you think you can is to make your personal daily habits a priority. It is important to first complete the items that cannot be done another day. You cannot put off exercise to another day. That other day requires exercise too. If you do not exercise today, the benefits are lost forever. This is true with all your positive daily habits—exercising, reading, praying, brushing your teeth, taking a vitamin—do these things first, and you will have an accomplished day. You can still do the laundry tomorrow, but once today is gone, some opportunities are lost forever. I know it sounds counterintuitive to spend time exercising, reading, and meditating when you have an overwhelming "to-do" list, but there is a miraculous thing that happens when you put those daily habits first. You will get more done. Time seems to magically appear, and you truly *can do more than you think you can.*

If it doesn't challenge you, it won't change you

Doing hard things is like strengthening a muscle. To strengthen a muscle, you must use enough weight and repetitions to challenge the muscle. Otherwise, you will not get stronger. It is the hard days, the days when you don't want to do it, but you do it anyway, that makes you stronger. You prove to yourself what you are made of on those days. Every time you overcome a challenge, you become stronger for the next one.

Road cycling is my passion. I love it! I used to regularly ride my bike to the top of a nearby mesa called Tablerock. I rode that mountain dozens of times every summer, and it was *always* hard. There was one hill, in particular, that was long and steep. Every time I rode that hill, I would tell myself I could go home if I wanted. No one was making me climb this hill. As soon as thoughts of quitting entered my head, I would replace them with, *I will do this or die trying!* I never turned around. That hill was always challenging, but it became a little less difficult the more I did it. It also made me stronger for other difficult things. I have used the inner strength, that I gained climbing that mountain on my bike, to do a myriad of other hard things: start a business, hold a plank or yoga pose, feed my family on a tight budget, get through a difficult pregnancy, train one more fitness class at the end of a long day, write a book, and sometimes just get up in the morning. When life is hard, think this: *If it doesn't challenge me, it won't change me.*

Staying strong in the middle is a life skill

Whether it is a hard minute, a hard hour, a hard day, or a hard life, it is in the middle that our challenge is the most difficult. The newness and excitement of what we have taken on have waned, or dwindled altogether, and the end seems so far away. Staying strong in the middle truly is a life skill, and it requires consistent application. Every time you give up when things become hard, it is easier to give up the next time. The opposite is also true. Every time you renew your commitment to stay strong in the middle, it is easier to stay strong the next time.

When you are struggling through something and feel tempted to quit, think of other times you persevered and prevailed. Remembering previous successes can give you the strength to accomplish new things. I was trying to master Dandayamana Janushirasana, or standing head to knee pose, in yoga some years ago. I assumed I was the only one in the class who couldn't master it, but I wasn't looking around to see how other people were doing. All of my energy was focused on balancing on one foot with my forehead resting on my extended leg. I could not hold the pose for more than a few seconds, and I was so frustrated! One day, I was in class, and I began to think about another hill on that road to Tablerock. I remembered how it was short but steep, had loose dirt and rocks that made the back tire of my bike slip, and how it sloped to the right, so if I drifted too far to that way, I would end up in the ditch. When I first started riding that hill, the sloping road was my biggest challenge because I felt like my bike was being pulled toward the ditch. I learned to get on the left side early and to fight gravity in order to stay there. If I did that, I always made it. Imagining my success on that hill, while working on that yoga pose, quickly gave me the confidence to master it. One day, I stopped and looked around the room at how others were doing. I was surprised to find I was the only class member that day who could do Dandayamana Janushirasana. When you are struggling in the middle, remember other successes and remind yourself *staying strong in the middle is a life skill.*

Finishing strong is a life skill

Have you ever been to a track meet and watched as a runner struggled toward the end of the race, then dug deep for one last surge of energy to sprint to the finish line? Whether the runner is first, last, or somewhere in the middle, the crowd cheers every time. We are inspired by that last surge of commitment to finish, and the harder the finish, the more inspiring it is. We are inspired by the competitor who finishes strong because *finishing strong is a life skill.*

For ten years, FitMania hosted a ninety-day fitness challenge two or three times per year. Besides our very intense fitness classes, we provided nutrition events and consultations, accountability coaching, tracking tools, and before/after pictures. We offered incentives, including vacation cruises and cash. In every challenge, I noticed a disturbing phenomenon: There would be at least one person who was killing it. They were on fire, and their results were proving it! They were progressing toward their previously unknown potential, and they were happy! Then, a peculiar thing would happen. A couple of weeks before the end of the challenge, an end in which they would be a contender for the big prize, they would quit. We are often more fearful of success than we are of failure, so perhaps that is why, or maybe because we are afraid of the pressure to live up to our success. Marianne Williamson suggested it is our light, not our darkness, that we fear most. In answering why some push for success and others give up, Jim Rohn said, "It is a mystery of the mind." It is certainly a mystery to me. For my staff and me, it was disappointing. For the client, the disappointment in themselves must have been bitter.

Sometimes finishing strong looks like a surge of energy at the end, and sometimes it looks like crawling toward the finish. The point is to give all you have and stay in the game until the end. *Finishing strong is a life skill.*

No excuses

You have probably seen NO EXCUSES on bumper stickers and t-shirts. It is a cliché, but a cliché tends to have some truth to it. So, grab hold of this one and repeat it often.

Fitness clients have given me all kinds of excuses for missing a workout. Most of our hundreds of clients could tell you my response to every excuse was, "Unless you are dead, or dying, bleeding profusely, or have a high fever, show up for your workout." It may sound heartless but drawing that kind of line in the sand was a gift to them because I understood a few things they had not yet learned. For example, the habit of working out is more important than the workout itself. And the habit is easy to lose. Once they miss a workout, they are 67% more likely to miss the next one. The workout they can barely finish will be one of the most important workouts they will ever do because of the discipline and confidence they will gain. Our brain, thinking it is protecting us, will look for reasons to miss a workout. To get clients in the door on days when they thought they couldn't work out, I would encourage them to come to the class anyway and watch. I assured them that coming to watch would help them reach their goals. Some came with the intention to sit through the workout, but to my knowledge, no one ever did. They might not have known it at the time, but their reasons were excuses. When they got to class, those excuses felt much smaller, and they realized they could do more than they thought they could, so they worked out. An excuse is worse than a lie. *No excuses.*

Never give up

Never give up on something that is worth completing. Frequently, the things you start are worth completing only because the other option is quitting and the biggest problem with quitting is how it becomes a habit. It is easier to quit the second time, and every time you quit, it is a little easier to quit again. When you start something and don't finish it, you strengthen the habit of quitting.

Surgery for weight loss is not something I support, except when I do. Anyone has the capacity to improve their diet, gain muscle, and lose fat. However, if a person starts and gives up enough times, the habit of quitting becomes so strong that it is impossible to overcome it and reach their fitness goals. At that point, weight loss surgery can become a matter of life or death. *Never give up. Ever.*

No regrets

There are a lot of reasons to *never give up,* but there are a lot of reasons to quit too, or at least it seems like it in the moment. When someone I care about wants to give up, I ask them what I ask myself: "If you quit, will you ever regret it? Living without regrets is a life skill."

Jumping off of cliffs and rocks into water is something I have done a lot, and I am afraid every time I jump. I love water, I love adventure, and I like a little thrill. I also know that if I don't jump, I will regret it later. To me, the feeling of regret is worse than the fear. So, I jump every time. One time, I almost didn't. It wasn't jumping in water, though. It was a ropes course in the mountains of Utah. I loved all the events that day until we got to one called the Eagle's Nest. You were required to climb a very tall lodgepole. It had wooden blocks on which to place your feet for most of the climb, and then the blocks changed to things that looked like large nails. On the top of the pole was a wooden platform about one-foot square. Getting onto that platform was tricky, but I accomplished that easily. Once I was standing on the platform, I was supposed to jump off and simultaneously grab a rubber chicken suspended some distance in front of me. This meant a leap forward as well. I was in a safety harness, and I had watched the others in my group successfully manage the whole thing, but I was frozen with fear! I do not know how long I stood up there, but it felt like forever. The members of my group were shouting encouragement and instruction, but there I stood. I knew if I didn't do this thing, I would regret it for the rest of my life. I gathered up all my courage and every bit of self-will I possessed, and I jumped. Even though I missed the chicken, I was proud of myself for jumping. And guess what? I was so happy! And not just because it was over! *No regrets.*

Remember your why

Fitness is a tough business. My years at FitMania were very intense and often discouraging. In interviews, or speaking at fund-raisers we sponsored, I would be asked questions like, "Why did you start FitMania?" or "What is your dream for FitMania?" or "What is your *why*?" I would always answer these questions the same way: "I know it sounds cheesy, but I want to change the world." Getting a grip on the physical self is critical to all personal development, and the world needed new ways of thinking about food and exercise. For most people, when they are vulnerable enough to admit it, the "pain point" isn't their health or even how they look to other people. It is the pain that comes from seeing oneself in the mirror, and knowing the image they see does not reflect who they are on the inside.

I felt if we could teach a few hundred people how to change, and if each of those people influenced the lives of a few people, and then those few influenced a few more, then we could change the world. I believe I achieved that goal. I have seen shifts in the fitness industry's thinking toward more natural ways of eating and moving, and I was one of those on the ground floor pushing for a better way. It was the second hardest thing I have ever done, and I paid a high price to do it. It was only, as Steve Jobs put it, a "dent in the universe," but the world is different because of my efforts. There are still plenty of people selling snake oil for fitness, but there is also an increasingly healthy approach to food and fitness. I had a small part in that. I still receive emails from people who thank me for providing a program that changed their lives. If I had forgotten my *why*, I would have missed putting this particular dent in the universe. *Remember your why.*

Here are nine simple power phrases to keep you motivated. Use them liberally.

- What you think about expands.
- You can always do more than you think you can.
- If it doesn't challenge you, it won't change you.
- Staying strong in the middle is a life skill.
- Finishing strong is a life skill.
- No excuses.
- Never give up.
- No regrets.
- Remember your why.

3

EXPANDING YOUR WHY

WHAT DO YOU REALLY WANT?

"Your purpose in life is to find your purpose and give your whole heart and soul to it."

~ Gautama Buddha ~

The business of personal development is a lot of day-to-day work. The desire for increased happiness is your ultimate *why*, but the desire for increased happiness will not always be enough to keep you focused on developing daily habits, setting and accomplishing goals, and dealing with failures. You must expand your *why* to make it so compelling you can't bear to quit, and then stay so focused on that *why* so failure is not even an option. When you feel the full extent of your *why*, your motivation will be so intense it will own your future such that the goals you set, the habits you develop, and your daily activities will be designed to be in alignment with your *why*.

One of the most intense trainings I ever participated in was an experiential personal development program. In the first level, we spent two-and-a-half days taking part in various activities designed to assist us in knowing who we were, what we wanted, and how to move forward. In one exercise, we spent three minutes with a partner asking us, "What do you want?" and "What do you really want?" and we would answer. Ignoring our answer, they continued asking the questions, over and over, increasing the intensity and demanding an answer. As we were asked these questions, we continued giving the same answer with increasing frustration. Three minutes of that is a long time, but toward the end of the three minutes, the weirdest thing happened. For most of the participants, the answers totally changed. Somewhere deep inside, most of us knew something we wanted, but until that moment, we had not consciously realized we wanted it, or how badly we wanted it. I later helped staff with some of these workshops, and this same phenomenon happened every time, with nearly every participant. Over the years, I have used this technique on myself by asking:

- What do I really want?
- What do I really want today?
- What do I really want this week?
- What do I really want in the next ninety days?
- What do I want out of life?

Ask yourself these questions with intensity and urgency. Once you have your answers, you will begin to know your *why*. We only have this one life, with only one chance to get it right! Know your *why* so you can live your life with no regrets.

There are some fortunate people who seem to be born knowing their *why*, but most of us will have to work at discovering our own. I do not know what your *why* will be, but if you want serious results, it has to be big. Daniel H. Burnham said, "Make no little plans; they have no magic to stir men's blood." Jim Collins and Jerry Porras coined the acronym BHAG in their 1994 book, *Built to Last: Successful Habits of Visionary Companies*. It stands for Big Hairy Audacious Goal. Your *why* must be compelling—a BHAG. A *why* such as "I want to be rich" or "I want to be thin" are not compelling enough to make you work when you'd rather not.

When my clients do not have a compelling *why,* they fail. At FitMania, people came in with goals like, "looking impressive for an upcoming class reunion" or "fitting into a certain sized wedding dress." Unless these people were committed to a fit lifestyle for other reasons, they didn't even make a good start. However, if I had a mom come in desperate to be healthy for her children, or a dad wanting to live long enough to raise his kids, or someone who felt their reflection in the mirror was not a reflection of who they truly are, or someone who simply wanted to be the kind of person who was fit as a way of life, then I knew they had a good chance at success. A *why* absolutely has to be compelling enough to carry us through the hard times.

Knowing happiness is the purpose of existence and *personal progression toward an infinite potential that is the key to happiness* is good information, but it isn't enough to ensure we will work for it. This chapter contains three tools to help you establish a decisive *why* to do the required work for personal progression:

1. The Big Dreams List
2. A Personal Mission Statement
3. Written Governing Values

THE BIG DREAMS LIST

"What great thing would you attempt if you knew you could not fail?"

~ Robert H. Schuller ~

To achieve a successful coaching experience, my clients must be excited about the possibilities for their lives. To facilitate this, one of the first things we do is build a Big Dreams list. The Big Dreams list is like a bucket list, except in a Big Dreams list, we also include things we want to *be* and to *have* in addition to things we want to *do.* However, things we want to *do* will typically make up most of our list. Creating a Big Dreams list is exciting and motivating. It expands our *why.* I require my Life Mastery clients to compile fifty items on their Big Dreams list before we proceed to the next skill.

You may have heard of the adventurer John Goddard. When John Goddard was fifteen years old, he wrote a list of goals he wanted to accomplish in his lifespan. This list included items from learning to type on a keyboard to climbing Mt. Everest. "When I was fifteen," he told *Life Magazine,* "all the adults I knew seemed to complain, 'Oh, if only I'd done this or that when I was younger.' They had let life slip by them. I was sure that if I planned for it, I could have a life of excitement and fun and knowledge." As a teenager, he wrote 127 goals. He ended up accomplishing over 100 of those original goals. He explored rivers like the Nile and the Congo, climbed mountains, learned to play musical instruments, composed music, studied primitive cultures, became an accomplished typist, taught college courses, became an Eagle Scout, served a mission for his church, married and had children, and maintained his weight at 175 pounds all his adult life—all goals he set at fifteen. A person like this doesn't stop adding to his list. Later in his life, he revealed to an acquaintance how the original list written by his fifteen-year-old self was just the beginning. He now had over 600 goals, and at that point, he had achieved 520 of them. John Goddard wrote his original list in 1940. One of the items on the list was to live into the twenty-first century. Goddard died in 2013, having lived a full life. I suspect he had very few regrets. Goddard once wrote the following:

> "From early childhood, I had always dreamed of becoming an explorer. Somehow I had acquired the impression that an explorer was someone who lived in the jungle with natives and lots of wild animals, and I couldn't imagine anything better than that! Unlike other little boys, most of whom changed their minds about what they want to be several times as they grew older, I never wavered from this ambition."

Write your own Big Dreams list. Do not limit your list by thinking something is impossible. John Goddard had "visit the moon" on his list. He didn't make that one, but he thought that big. Make each item on your list specific. For example, do not write "visit Europe" but list each country, city, monument, fountain, and museum. Make each item on your list quantifiable. Rather than "read more classics," choose a number like "read one hundred classics books." List languages you want to learn, people you want to meet, sporting events you want to attend, skills you want to learn, and objects you would like to possess. Do not worry if you struggle to get to fifty at first. Once it is on your mind, you will begin thinking of new items to add, and in the process of accomplishing one, you will think of two more.

Goals such as "My son is a lawyer," or "My wife is a size six," or "My mother quits smoking" are off-limits. You cannot have Big Dreams for someone else. However, if you have a life companion, you may want to compare Big Dreams and see what you want to do together. If you have children, sharing your Big Dreams lists is a great family activity. I had a client who struggled coming up with his own Big Dreams list. Immediately after one of our meetings, he left for a family road trip with his wife and teenagers. I encouraged him to brainstorm ideas with his family while they drove. He later reported the discussion had been a great success. He completed his list, and his kids had so much fun they want to do it again.

When I first started my Big Dreams list, I would delete items when I accomplished them. I am appalled that I did that! Now, I put a little check by the dreams accomplished. If you do something awesome and it wasn't on your list, add it and mark it off. Our daughter, Summer, keeps two Big Dreams lists. One is her *To-Do* list, and one is her *Done* list. Make sure you keep a record of all you have done. One thing you might want to do that I didn't think of soon enough is to add the date when you accomplish an item.

My list now has many items accomplished, a few things in the works, and a lot left to do. Because accomplishing one goal gives rise to other Big Dreams, I expect to be adding more items to my list. This is how it looks now:

1. X 100 memorized scriptures
2. X Read the standard works
3. ___ Read all my leather-bound books
4. ___ Be interviewed in a national forum
5. ___ Speak in my hometown
6. ___ Speak on a cruise
7. X New York City
8. X Paris
9. X Washington, D.C.
10. X Washington, D.C., on July 4th
11. X Martha's Vineyard
12. X Croatia
13. X Portugal
14. X France
15. X Italy
16. X Switzerland
17. X Netherlands
18. X Belgium
19. X Spain
20. X Germany
21. X Morocco
22. X Thailand
23. X Caribbean cruise
24. X European cruise
25. X Alaskan cruise
26. X South American cruise
27. X Ecuador
28. X Belize
29. X Mexico
30. X Guatemala
31. X Columbia
32. X Costa Rica
33. X Panama
34. X Argentina
35. X Falkland Island
36. X Uruguay
37. ___ Scotland
38. ___ England
39. ___ Wales
40. ___ Sweden
41. ___ Finland
42. X Israel
43. X Jordan
44. ___ Greece
45. ___ China
46. X New Zealand
47. X Australia
48. X Aruba
49. X Turk Islands
50. X Grand Cayman
51. X Puerto Rico
52. X St Thomas
53. X St. Marteen
54. X Dominica
55. X Fiji
56. X Banff, Canada
57. X Glacier National Forest
58. X Yellowstone Nat'l Forest w/Ken
59. X Redwood National/State Forest
60. ___ Galapagos Islands
61. ___ Egyptian pyramids
62. X Mayan Pyramids
63. ___ African Safari
64. ___ Cycle through New England
65. X Cycle to Idaho City
66. X Cycle around Lake Tahoe
67. X Cycle Hiawatha Trail
68. X Visit every continent
69. ___ Visit 100 countries
70. X Visit all 50 states
71. ___ Broadway play in NY
72. X Swim in Dead Sea
73. X See the Rockettes
74. X Take a week scuba trip w/Gigi
75. ___ Scuba dive Red Sea

76. X See Petra
77. X Run a 5K
78. X Run a 10K
79. X Do 50 regulation pushups in 1 minute
80. X Do a triathlon sprint
81. X Run obstacle course event
82. ___ Sailboat the Mediterranean
83. ___ Sailboat the Caribbean
84. X Hike Mt Borah
85. X See Hells Canyon
86. X See Silver City
87. X Raft the Salmon River (overnight)
88. X Hike Tour du Mont Blanc
89. ___ Walk Portugal
90. ___ Walk Scotland
91. ___ Travel the Amazon
92. ___ Overnight train ride
93. X Ride a camel (native)
94. X Ride an elephant (native)
95. ___ World Series game
96. X Pro Baseball game
97. ___ Pro football game
98. X Pro basketball game
99. ___ Hockey game
100. ___ Olympic event
101. X Take my kids on a cruise
102. X Own a gun
103. X Take handgun training
104. ___ Proficient at genealogy
105. X Cash for a new Mercedes
106. X Leave a $100 tip
107. X Live in a downtown condo
108. ___ Hot air balloon ride
109. ___ Helicopter Grand Canyon
110. ___ Turn $200 into $10,000
111. X Own a fitness business
112. X Develop a personal development coaching program
113. X Write a workbook for *Life Mastery*
114. X Write an assessment for use in Life Mastery
115. ___ Publish a book on Life Mastery
116. ___ Publish a book of quotes
117. ___ Sell 10,000 copies quote book
118. ___ Attend Jewish Seder
119. ___ Attend Catholic Mass
120. X Learn fly fishing
121. X Attend a ballet
122. ___ Attend an opera
123. X Study the ruins of Belize
124. ___ Skydive
125. X Take Isaac on a super trip
126. X Take Brady on a super trip
127. X Take Brock on a super trip
128. X Take Sam on a super trip
129. X Take Rachel on a super trip
130. ___ Take Ian on a super trip
131. ___ Take Lilly on a super trip
132. ___ Take Maya on a super trip
133. ___ Take Ella on a super trip
134. ___ Take Carson on a super trip
135. ___ Take Cora on a super trip
136. ___ Take Lidia on a super trip
137. ___ Take Emmy on a super trip
138. ___ Take Jude on a super trip
139. ___ Take Jase on a super trip
140. ___ Take Zach on a super trip
141. ___ Take Blythe on a super trip
142. ___ Take GeorgeAndrew on a super trip
143. X Take granddaughters trail riding
144. X Participate in a bodybuilding show

You do not have to love something to have it be worth your time. Do it for the experience. Watching sporting events is not a favorite activity of mine, but it is a huge part of our culture, and I don't want to miss out. It turns out I have enjoyed the sporting events I have attended and didn't need the book I had stowed in my purse in case I was bored. The philosopher Bertrand Russell thought people should be interested in many things: "The more things a man is interested in, the more opportunities of happiness he has." This fits nicely with our quest for happiness through personal growth.

Recently, I asked myself what items on my list I would most regret not completing. One item instantly sprang to mind. It was something I had deleted. I had always wanted to participate in the figure division of a bodybuilding competition. In my fifties, I decided I was too old to lose enough body fat to compete with much younger women, so I deleted it. However, I knew if I didn't get on that stage, I would regret it. I put "participate in a bodybuilding show" back on my list. I still didn't want to lose an extreme amount of body fat, but my goal had always been to participate in a show, not necessarily win one, so a single-digit body fat percentage wasn't warranted. And they now have divisions for older women. Getting on that stage was one of the hardest things I have ever done, but I am happy to report I completed that Big Dream. I was the oldest woman in the show, and in way over my head, but I am pleased with myself for having done it. I might do another one to see if I can do a little better now that I know more. *No regrets.*

Having an inspiring and exciting Big Dreams list is one big *why* to do all the daily, weekly, yearly, sometimes prosaic activities necessary to make those dreams a reality.

A PERSONAL MISSION STATEMENT

"Without a mission statement, you might get to the top of the ladder, and then realize it was leaning against the wrong building."

~ Dave Ramsey ~

A Big Dreams list is exciting, but it is only one leg of the prover-bial three-legged stool. It doesn't stand alone in providing the *why* behind the work of personal growth.

Every one of us has unique gifts and talents. We develop some, and we bring others into the world with us. Ken and I have six children, and I have always been amazed at how six humans, from the same gene pool, could be so totally different. They were different from their very first breaths. It doesn't take long with a new baby to see what their gifts are and what their struggles are going to be. Each of us has a responsibility to discover our own gifts and find a way to use those gifts to make the world a better place. There is no neutral ground in the universe. We are either a drain on the planet, or we are contributing to a better world. A clear picture of what we have to offer, and how we will offer it, will ensure we are in the latter category.

In 2007, Ken and I had a plan. We were often traveling, and when we were home, Ken worked about three days a week. Our plan was for Ken to be mostly retired, just checking in from time to time, so we could travel for longer periods of time. We planned a supported bike ride from coast to coast across the United States, and after that, we would do some service missions. Then the recession hit. When the building industry went from boom to bust in 2008, we owned a construction supply business with multiple locations. That business was our golden goose, and it was in trouble. To make matters worse, two of our locations were in resort areas. We had properties to make payments on and employees to take care of. It looked like we would lose everything. Ken went back to work to save our business.

Our son Andrew, the youngest of our six children, had just graduated high school and was living on his own. First, we sold our large home and moved into a small condo. This freed up cash to support our business. Ken was working long hours. Because our plan had been to travel for the next few years, I had not made plans for an enterprise of my own, and my skills and talents do not translate well into the construction supply business. We had an entirely different life than what we had planned, but I was happy. I actually marveled at how I could lose so much and hardly feel it. I was using my time to think, read, and wander. A little bit of wandering is good, but my personal mission in this life is not to wander—it's to use my talents to make a difference. Other than teaching a class once a week and speaking on rare occasions, I wasn't living my mission like I thought I should. I needed a place where I could teach what I knew. So in December 2009, smack dab in the middle of a recession, I opened a fitness boutique and called it FitMania.

When I told my dad about my new adventure, he was incredulous. He asked me why I would want to start a business at this point in my life. He expressed his strong opinion that I had worked hard and should drive around in my convertible, play with my grandchildren, and enjoy my easy life. There were two reasons I couldn't do that. The first is that I have a need to build and nurture. The second, and more important reason, is that I have a mission. I believe strongly in the potential of humans, and I believe I have the ability to empower people to reach and grow toward that potential. My mission was clear because twenty-five years earlier, after much consideration, I wrote my Mission Statement. I had been using it to help me make decisions for all of those years. This is my Mission Statement: *I use all the knowledge, wisdom, and personal power I possess to empower others in their personal progression toward their infinite potential.*

A mission statement is helpful in making big decisions such as choosing careers, but can also be useful in moment-to-moment decisions. For example, I frequently find myself in the grocery store at the end of a long day. I am tired, hungry, and I want to go home, but I need food for tomorrow. The person scanning my groceries is also at the end of a long day. I don't feel like talking, but my mission is to empower people, and this person in front of me could use a kind word. So, I gather the energy to pay a compliment or say some words of gratitude for their service to me. I hope it empowers them in some way, but I will never know.

There is an old story often told about a boy who is walking along the beach. The beach is strewn with thousands of starfish, which have washed ashore. As he walks along, he throws as many starfish as he can back into the water, and hopefully to safety. After watching the boy for a time, a man asks the boy how he possibly hopes to make a difference when there are so many starfish on the beach. As the boy throws a starfish back into the sea, he says, "It makes a difference to this one." The traditional moral of the story is good enough but consider this: Maybe the starfish is saved, or maybe it is already dead. Who could tell with a starfish? Maybe it will just wash ashore again with the next tide. Regardless of the fate of the starfish, the effort is not lost. The boy has become better because of his effort to save a few starfish. The universe seems designed to keep us from knowing the effects of our actions on others. Every time we dig a little deeper, stretch when we don't want to, and live our mission, we grow a tiny bit and become a little happier.

A Mission Statement is a short statement you can memorize and quickly bring to mind. It is a statement of what your gifts are, and what you will do with them to make the world a better place. You might ask yourself the question Fredrick Buechner posed: "At what point do my talents and deep gladness meet the world's deep need?" That question alone might give you a Mission Statement, but most people need a little more help. When I work with clients in forming their own mission statement, I use this little formula:

1. Divide a piece of paper into three vertical columns. Title the first column, "My Unique Gifts," head the second column "Action," and the third column "Result."
2. Under "My Unique Gifts," list as many of your own personal gifts and talents as possible. Ask supportive people who care about you what things they see in you and include them on

your list. Think of compliments and kind things people have said to you over the years. If you have heard something more than once or twice, assume it is true even if you do not feel it. This will probably be your longest list.

3. Your shortest list might be the middle column. Under "Action," write verbs that speak to your talents such as teach, lead, guide, inspire, empower, and uplift.

4. Under "Result," write the ways you would like to influence people's lives. What would you want for others? Would you have people be more passionate, see their own potential, live with purpose, be happier, have faith, or find their own gifts? Perhaps you would bring comfort or lift burdens. Your list might look something like this:

My Unique Gifts	Action	Result
Compassion	Teach	Live with passion
Intelligence	Inspire	Develop talent
Wisdom	Serve	See potential
Kindness	Empower	Ease burdens
Artistic	Lead	Bring peace
Listening		Strengthen families
Faith		
Knowledge		
Nurturing		

5. Now thoughtfully, and with much consideration, narrow down your list of gifts to three items or less.

6. Next, look at your third column and decide how you would most like to serve the world with your gifts. Choose one to three items from your list.

7. Then, choose the action word that will best use your gifts to create your purpose.

8. Now, link the words in order to form a sentence. Make it concise enough so it is easy to remember. For example, "With all the wisdom and kindness I possess, I will serve others to ease their burdens." Every word you choose should

be a strong word. Make sure each word evokes a powerful emotion in you.

Every time you say or read your mission statement, it should make you feel powerful or excited. You may need to test it for a while. I suggest you print it and put it up in a place where you will see it often. Notice if there are words you wince at a bit. Does the phrase empower you? This format is an exercise to get you started. Change the format if it works better for you. The meaning of words is personal, and it only matters what each word means to you. It also only matters what your Mission Statement means to you. Write it without consideration of what other people might think. Only share it with people you feel safe with.

Some people I have coached find their Mission Statement immediately. Others will work on it for months. Eventually, you may find a short version that works. My brother-in-law put *MAKE A DIFF* (make a difference) on his vanity license plate. I worked with a young artistic woman who had a simple mission statement that said, "I will bring beauty to the world." The short version for me is *I empower others*. The short version of your Mission Statement will come after using the longer version for so long, that your brain fills in the full meaning.

You may discover a better word to express your statement, and you will certainly use your mission in different arenas throughout your life, but the fundamental mission will never change. I do not foresee a time when I will not be living my mission statement in some way because a Mission Statement is not what you do—it is who you are. When it comes to living your mission statement, you will feel like Richard Machowicz; *Not Dead—Can't Quit.*

WRITTEN GOVERNING VALUES

"When your values are clear to you, making decisions is easier."

~ Roy Disney ~

A Big Dreams list generates excitement about all the possibilities in the world; all the things there are to see, do, learn, and possess. A Personal Mission Statement is about the obligation to use your gifts to make the world a better place. It gives depth to your *why*. Governing Values is the last piece. It is a written personal constitution of what you value. It is based on who you are and who you are becoming. Governing Values form an internal compass that directs your *why*.

When my children were young, we listened to a fictional audiobook about Benjamin Franklin. In the story, Ben Franklin is transported, at the end of his life, to the twentieth century. He has many adventures in twentieth-century America, but the one that has stuck with me is when he attends a college lecture about himself. The lecturer is rehearsing all of the excesses and less desirable qualities Franklin, by his own admission, was known to have. After listening for some time, he becomes indignant and defensive. *Utterly amazing,* thinks Franklin. *Because I had confessed such follies from my youth, was I to be judged a slave to such vices throughout my life? Apparently, in the eyes of history, there was no such thing as repentance or rectification. The man at eighteen was the same man at eighty?*[3]

Older is not always wiser. It is possible for someone to be eighty years old and not necessarily be any better a person than he was at eighteen. But Benjamin Franklin did get wiser. Early in his life, a friend of Franklin's told him no one liked him, and that conversation was the impetus for his desire to change. He decided he wanted to be a better man, and had an idea of what he wanted that to look like, so he wrote down thirteen "virtues" he aspired to:

---

[3]   Chris Heimerdinger, *Ben Franklin and the Chamber of Time* (Salt Lake City: Deseret Book Co., 1995), 116.

1. Temperance: Eat not to dullness; drink not to elevation.
2. Silence: Speak not but what may benefit others or yourself; avoid trifling conversation.
3. Order: Let all your things have their places; let each part of your business have its time.
4. Resolution: Resolve to perform what you ought; perform without fail what you resolve.
5. Frugality: Make no expense but to do good to others or yourself. Waste nothing.
6. Industry: Lose no time; be always employed in something useful; cut off all unnecessary actions.
7. Sincerity: Use no hurtful deceit; think innocently and justly, and, if you speak, speak accordingly.
8. Justice: Wrong none by doing injuries or omitting the benefits that are your duty.
9. Moderation: Avoid extremes; forbear resenting injuries so much as you think they deserve.
10. Cleanliness: Tolerate no uncleanliness in body, clothes, or habitation.
11. Tranquility: Be not disturbed at trifles, or at accidents common or unavoidable.
12. Chastity: Rarely use venery but for health or offspring, never to dullness, weakness, or the injury of your own or another's peace or reputation.
13. Humility: Imitate Jesus and Socrates.

Franklin would take a single virtue at a time, work on it for a week, and then move on to the next. At the end of thirteen weeks, he would begin again. He also reviewed all thirteen virtues daily, and—this is worth noting—he reviewed his day and tracked his progress.

There is a parable that tells a similar story in *The Greatest Salesman in the World* by Og Mandino. The story is of a man who went from the lowly position of camel-driver to the richest and most successful salesman in the world. The secret to his success was the reading and practicing of twelve scrolls, or virtues, written beautifully and with much detail. These are different virtues than Franklin's, but like Franklin's, they are a personal constitution designed to govern one's own behavior.

Hyrum Smith is the founder of the Franklin Institute, now known as The FranklinCovey Company. The use of "Franklin" in the company name is a nod to Benjamin Franklin, whose many personal development practices influenced their day-planner system. I first heard Hyrum Smith use Governing Values to describe a personal constitution when I heard him speak decades ago. Later I read his book, *The 10 Natural Laws of Successful Time and Life Management*. That book was instrumental in helping me write my own Governing Values.

In the 1970s, factories that made motor homes and camp trailers hired hundreds of young people in Southwest Idaho. I worked as a draftsman in one of these factories. While working there, I met a long-haired man who also worked at the same factory. He had been traveling around the country in a Volkswagen van, and Boise is where he ran out of money. He was living day-to-day and planning on going back to California. He drank too much, used a few drugs, and lived in an old beat-up single-wide trailer. I must have seen the potential, because I married that long-haired man, and I have had a front-row seat as he became a man any woman would be proud to be married to. More remarkable than his financial and business success is who he became as a person. He is a respected businessman, a respected leader in his church, and in his community, and most especially, loved by his family. He is a person of great accomplishment and integrity.

To write Governing Values is not enough. You must have a plan for living them. Hyrum Smith wrote, "Your governing values should be important enough to you that you will invest your time, resources, and energy in making them a fundamental part of your life." Years ago, Ken read about Franklin's virtues and Og Mandino's scrolls. He wrote his own list, long before we called them Governing Values, and he worked at living them for years. When I thought my fabulous husband could not get much better, he upped his game using his Governing Values. I asked him to share his story:

"Sherry and I did a three-day retreat at the end of last year. She went her way, and I went my way. Spending three days, alone, just working on myself without any outside distractions, was an amazing opportunity. My number one goal was to really get my Governing Values refined. I came home with ten well-thought-out, well-defined, written Governing Values. I began on January first to take one Governing Value each month and work on it. Three times a day, morning, mid-day, and before I go to bed, I read the current one out loud. Each value is written out in detail and about a page long. It might take me two to three minutes to go through it. That is about ten minutes of my day. This process helps me to remember that value, and I become more consciously aware.

When you live with someone, it is difficult to notice any change day-to-day, but I had only been using this system for a short time when Sherry told me she could see a positive change in me. I have read, and studied, about the value of written daily goals and/or daily affirmations for years. I have tried different approaches to doing this with mixed results, mostly positive, but the progress was slower than I wanted. Now the change was coming so rapidly that even my wife could see it in me. I could feel it in myself. I told Sherry, one day, not long after that conversation, that I felt that I was the best version of myself that I had ever been.

There is a gap between how we are living our lives and what we know. The narrower the gap, the happier we are. I have been narrowing that gap at a faster pace than I ever have in my life. And guess what? I am happier today than I have ever been in my life. The reason for that is, the personal progress that I am making through using my Governing Values daily. I can't begin to tell you what a difference it has made in my life. We are programmed to react to stimuli in our lives; without thinking, we just react. I love this quote by Victor Frankl: 'Between stimulus and response, there is a space; in that space is our freedom to choose our response; in our response lies our growth and our freedom.' Just think how powerful it would be to become a person who always thinks before reacting, never regretting what we said. The beauty of this is, that in time these governing values will help me become that person. I will no longer have to stop and think about my reaction; my reaction will be motivated by those values. I will close the gap on what I know and who I am."

Ken is drawn more to the descriptive flare of Og Mandino's scrolls than Benjamin Franklin's virtues. My favorite of his Governing Values is the one about me, of course, but this is my second favorite:

I Live My Life with Joy

My life is as blessed a life as a person can possibly have. I know God and His love for me. I have a beautiful relationship with my wife, Sherry. I have six amazing children and twenty wonderful grandchildren whom I love, and they love me. I have a strong, healthy body. I live in a free democracy where I have the freedom to choose my life. I am financially independent. I have a strong, clear mind with the ability to learn and grow. I have been blessed with a strong motivation to always improve. If I am that blessed and still don't feel joy every day, I don't deserve these blessings. *I live my life with joy.*

I have gratitude in my heart for the blessed life that I have. I smile and laugh easily. I tell the world, by my attitude, how joyful I really am. I will not just feel that joy on the inside; I will show it to people wherever I go. Never has a man been blessed more abundantly than I have. The scriptures say, "Adam fell that man might be, and men are that they might have joy." We are not put on this earth to suffer through it in misery until we once again meet our God. No, God has given us this beautiful world with amazing people, so that we can live a joyful life. *I live my life with joy.*

There will be sad times in my life; that is a part of this mortal probation. I will weep over these sad events. But I know that these trials are a part of God's plan and that I will grow closer to Him because of them. During those sad times, I will stop and reflect on the blessings in my life. Then I will remember that *I live my life with joy.*

When I wrote my own Governing Values, I felt I needed to include the three relationships closest to me. My first value concerns my relationship with God, the second with my husband, and the third my role as a mother. Other than those three, they are not in any particular order. A concise statement of each Governing Value works best for me:

My Governing Values

1. I have a personal relationship with God.
2. I hold my marriage sacred.
3. I hold motherhood sacred.
4. I am consistently improving.
5. I live my personal mission.
6. I am a leader.
7. I love people.
8. I am outward-focused.
9. I am disciplined.
10. I am grateful.
11. I am happy.

The writing of Governing Values will be a unique process to you, and your end result will be even more unique, but here are a few ideas to get you started:

- Find some time alone where you will not be interrupted.
- List the character traits you most value (you might find some help identifying those things in Part II: What).
- Read the full story of Benjamin Franklin's quest for improvement and *The Greatest Salesman in the World*. The FranklinCovey company can also be a resource for writing your own Governing Values.
- Consider writing them in the first person and as if they are already so. For example: "I live my life with joy" or "I am the master of my emotions."
- Plan a system of action to implement your Governing Values in your life.

The world offers so much to see and do. A Big Dreams list is a place to record the options we choose for ourselves. To be in the best position possible to live our big dreams, we have a reason, a *why*, to take care of our body, our relationships, and our finances. A Personal Mission Statement reminds us we also have a responsibility to give back and provides motivation and direction, or a *why*, to maximize our gifts for the good of others. Written Governing Values is a personal constitution of who we aspire to be, and a *why* to work on becoming that person. Remember, our universal, ultimate why is to be happy, and as we do more, serve with more focus, and become a better human being, we find we are happier. *Why?* Because *personal progression toward an infinite potential is the key to happiness.*

PART II

WHAT

The following eight chapters are not meant to be totally comprehensive on each topic. They are designed to give you enough information to start you thinking about your goals. As you read these chapters, keep a notebook nearby, or write goal ideas that appeal to you in the margins of the pages. Do not worry about the goal being too hard or even impossible. Also, take time to write an answer to the reflective questions at the end of each of these chapters. Your notes on ideas for goals and your answers to the reflective questions will be invaluable to you when you start implementing the practices in Part III: How.

We often refer to people who are financially successful as simply successful. However, the truly successful person must achieve more than that. One instance of this is a man I know who is extremely successful in business. He is innovative, creative, and world-class in his field, but he is less fit than he knows he could be. He is self-conscious about his appearance, and it adversely affects his happiness, as well as his feelings of accomplishment.

In another example, there was a woman who once had a beautiful marriage. The husband had been told repeatedly, by his doctor, that he needed to make some changes to his diet and lifestyle. He was already experiencing some health problems and was in danger of suffering a stroke. He refused to make changes, and when I met them, he was disabled from the predicted stroke. Because of his unwillingness to make changes, she became his caregiver for decades. She began to resent him for the increased responsibility she had to care for him, the lost opportunities to travel, and the loss of his companionship. I watched over the years as her love faded and her resentment grew.

To be successful in our physical health alone is not to be a successful person. There are people who are so addicted to fitness and high adventure that their relationships suffer, and their finances are always strained. To be very successful in one arena and to be failing in another is not a success. The Life Mastery areas are eight major areas of life. Without success in these high-impact areas, there is no fullness of happiness. To have a fullness of happiness, we must have mastery of each of these eight areas:

- Physical
- Spiritual
- Relationships
- Education
- Money
- Vocation
- Lifestyle
- Character

If I were reading this book and I was not already implementing these Life Mastery Skills, I would feel overwhelmed with the amount of time it would take to progress in all the ways suggested. It does take time, but rather than allow yourself to be discouraged, get excited about the possibilities. You have more time than you think, and *you are not using your time the way you think you are.* If you want to prove it to yourself, track your time for three days. You can use a smartphone app to help you do it. While you do have more time than you think you do, life is also shorter than you think, and you really don't have time to waste. In Part III: How, I will give you some tools to help you set, organize, manage, and track your goals. These tools will make it feel less overwhelming. In the meantime, remember *you can always do more than you think you can.*

4

LIFE MASTERY AND THE PHYSICAL SELF

PHYSICAL TRANSFORMATION IS A TEACHER

"Physical fitness is not only one of the most important keys to a healthy body, it is the basis of dynamic and creative intellectual activity."

~ John F. Kennedy ~

Amazing body transformations were a normal part of our workday experience at FitMania. As the lifestyles of our clients changed, the rest of their lives began to follow. We saw relationships restored, household debt paid off, and dreams achieved as clients began to believe in themselves. They applied what they had learned from their physical transformations to the rest of their lives. These people were energized, excited about life, and so happy! Our FitMania team would often ask each other, "What could we be doing that would be more satisfying than watching these clients' lives change and being a part of it?" With all the happiness that comes with personal change, FitMania was a very happy place, and the years I spent there was a privilege.

Throughout this book, I have used many experiences from physical fitness to illustrate points I want to make. Physical goals are easy to track and measure. FitMania clients, who began experiencing real results in their fitness levels, wanted to take their newly found self-discipline to the other areas of their personal development. Their eagerness to improve made these people a delight to work with. In Life Mastery Coaching, I work with clients individually and without the benefit of time at FitMania. I have found that those who still need to develop mastery of their physical selves will frequently require an inordinate amount of time discussing issues with food, fitness, self-image, body image, and lack of self-discipline. These clients will typically need coaching for a longer period of time.

The physical is easy to see, easy to manage, relate to, and use for great metaphors. Who doesn't love a good sports analogy? Or movies about teams and people who persevere to win? The physical is a good place to develop the skills and principles needed for success and happiness. It is also why, out of the eight areas of personal development, I start with the physical.

TAKE CHARGE OF YOUR OWN HEALTH

"Every human being is the author of his own health or disease."

~ Buddha ~

When she was two weeks old, it was discovered our granddaughter, Emmy, had two problems with her heart. She was taken by helicopter to Salt Lake City, where they took that tiny little heart out of her body, repaired it, and put it back in. She is now a super active and delightful nine-year-old. There are times when surgeries and medications are necessary, and I am in awe of what masters of modern medicine can do, but they cannot protect us from ourselves.

We are an indulgent society, and while this is hardly unique in the history of the world, what is unique about our society is just how many things we have to indulge in. Most diseases that kill us now are chronic diseases caused or influenced by lifestyle rather than the acute diseases that killed our ancestors. The majority of our healthcare dollars are spent on these illnesses. One out of every nine people over sixty-five will get Alzheimer's, and Alzheimer's has been linked to lifestyle choices, as has type II diabetes, cardiovascular diseases, addictions, HIV, cancer, and obesity-related illnesses. Viruses, like the common cold and flu, are also influenced by the choices we make. If you want to have mastery over your own life and to be happy, do not leave your health and wellness to someone else. It is not McDonald's problem if you eat too many fries, or Nabisco's fault you have an Oreo addiction. It is not Netflix that makes you sit on the couch. Too many people are like Humpty Dumpty—their lifestyle causes their great fall, they expect doctors to put them back together, and they want insurance or tax dollars to pay for it. Then they complain because the cracks show.

I love to wear sexy, strappy, high-heeled shoes. My good friend, Randy, is an excellent podiatrist. Randy shakes his head and tells me, "Keep wearing those shoes, and I will fix your feet later." It's fun to wind him up, and I like the friendly banter, so I don't let on that I wear them less than he thinks. I am also careful about how my shoes fit, so I don't plan on needing him to fix my feet. But Randy's remarks about fixing my feet later struck a chord. Too many people have an *I will do as I please now and fix it later* approach to health.

Movement cures. Mental, emotional, and physical conditions can be positively influenced, or cured, with purposeful, focused movement. Anxiety and depression are ubiquitous in our modern society. People with these conditions are automatically prescribed medication, even though both anxiety and depression have been proven to respond at least as well to moderate or intense exercise, and there are no negative side effects to movement.

Regularly, I encountered people who were advised to have knee surgery but chose to continue working out instead. They kept moving the best they could, and after a few months, they were better. Clients came through our doors with appointments scheduled for surgery, looking for a last-chance solution. One woman in her sixties, who loved to run, came into FitMania looking for a solution to her back problem. She had already had several back surgeries and was told she needed another one. I suggested she try our program for a few months first. She took my suggestion and never did have that surgery.

One of my favorite examples of movement curing a condition was a young father named Mario. He had wanted to work out with us for two years, but his doctors discouraged him because of back pain. Since nothing else was helping, he decided to try working out with us anyway. It wasn't long before he was rocking the workouts, and in a few months, he was doing front planks with his feet on the wall, which takes a very strong back. It doesn't always happen like that, but it happens often enough to be disturbing. If you ask a *surgeon* for advice, then they will likely suggest surgery. That is what they are trained for, so they are biased toward that course of action. If you ask your general practitioner for advice, you will likely receive a prescription. It isn't that these answers are always wrong, but they are not always right either. Our health is our own responsibility. We must do our research, consider our options, trust our instincts, and trust our body to take care of us if we take care of it.

EAT AND TRAIN

"The only time to eat diet food is while you're waiting for the steak to cook."

~ Julia Child ~

Are you as tired of the phrases *diet and exercise* and *weight loss* as I am? The *weight loss* industry (and it is a huge industry) has trained us to look for instant results and focus on *thinness*. Most diet programs will make you *thinner,* but the effects don't last, and the end result can be worse than in the beginning. It hurts my heart when people go on a diet, lose weight, and when they inevitably gain that weight back, they blame themselves. They believe they lost their beautiful new body because they just didn't have enough self-discipline. If you have been through lose-gain cycles, let me assure you the problem is not your self-discipline! If you can stay on a diet, you have incredible discipline! The problem is inherent in the dieting process. One of the many problems with diets is how they are not sustainable. Once the diet is over, and it's time to eat normally, you fall back to your old habits because it is all you know. Your body changed, but YOU didn't.

Athletes don't *diet and exercise*. Athletes *eat and train*. Athletes *eat and train* so they can be *lean and strong*. To an athlete, the body is not a burden to be subdued, but a gift to be cared for. You are an athlete on the playing field of life, and the more fit you are, the better you will play. In this section, there will be no recommendation of a *diet* program, or any further uses of phrases like *weight loss* and *exercise*. We are looking to be *lean* (a healthy amount of body fat) and *fit* (strong muscles, bones, heart, lungs, feet, and good balance and agility). This is not a short-term project so you can look good at the beach in twelve weeks. To be *lean and fit* requires healthy daily habits *for the rest of your life*. Because you will be an athlete on the playing field of life, you will need to *eat and train* all of your life. Attaining and retaining a lean and strong body is assured by developing the right daily habits and practicing them forever.

Everyone wants to look good, but there are many more benefits to being fit than just looking good in your jeans. A lifestyle of fitness means a lifetime of good health. Healthy people...

- Are more successful
- Are happier
- Have better sex lives
- Have more energy
- Sleep better
- Make better first impressions
- Find higher quality mates
- Spend less on healthcare
- Live longer

You do not have to arrive at some magic level of leanness and fitness before you start seeing these results. The advantages begin as soon as the habits become part of who you are, and you are a person who is *always* getting better.

REAL FOOD REAL OFTEN

"There are no new fundamentals. You've got to be a little suspicious of someone who says, 'I've got a new fundamental.'"

~ Jim Rohn ~

It is frustrating to see nearly every conversation about food framed in the context of the best foods for decreasing or increasing body fat. Food is not only necessary to live, it's a joyous part of a beautiful life. Food is not the enemy. Food is not a problem.

It took me decades to figure out how to eat to be lean. I tried the rice diet, where the theory was that in Asian cultures, people were typically thin, and they ate a lot of rice; ergo, rice would make you thin. I tried the cabbage diet, where I made a big batch of soup made from cabbage and a few other vegetables. I ate the soup for two meals a day, along with a "normal" dinner. The soup tasted good, but it didn't take long to get tired of it. It was also so low in calories that I thought I might starve to death. When I periodically tried the "just don't eat anything!" diet, I might truly have starved had biology not kicked in. Not eating enough is like holding your breath. Eventually, you have to come up for air, and when you do, you gulp in all you can hold. Like many people, I fell for too many "snake oil" salesmen, fame-seekers, fads, and sincere but misguided "experts" who obscured both the problem and the solution. The problem *isn't how much you eat*—it's **what** you eat and **when** you eat *it*. The solution:

Eat real food real often

EAT LIKE A TRUCK

"To a significant degree, we are an overfed and undernourished nation digging an early grave with our teeth, and lacking the energy that could be ours."

~ Ezra Taft Benson ~

We own a company called Concrete Construction Supply. Our employees deliver products to our customers and transport products among our six locations. This requires a fleet of trucks. Some of these trucks use gas for fuel, and some use diesel. Occasionally, a driver will accidentally put gasoline in a diesel-engine truck. That truck will immediately begin to run poorly, and then quit running completely, until it is repaired. The procedure to repair a diesel truck that has been filled with gasoline is to flush the fuel system with clean diesel. *It is literally repaired with the fuel it was designed to use.* In the world we live in, people use all kinds of *foods* for fuel, but a lot of it is like gasoline in a diesel engine.

Fuel for humans is pretty simple: *If it doesn't grow from the ground, hang from a tree, or have a parent, do not put it in your mouth.* If every ingredient does not fit those criteria, do not buy it and do not eat it. Food should also be eaten whole, meaning that it is not separated from its other parts. For example, fruit juice being separated from the pulp, egg whites being separated from the yolks, or milk being separated from the fat.

Just as the diesel engine is repaired by flushing it with the right fuel, the solution to obesity, as well as many other of our physical, mental, and emotional problems, is found by filling ourselves with the nutrient-dense fuel we were designed to eat. No one becomes obese by eating broccoli, apples, turnips, steak, or any of the other foods we were designed to eat. Highly processed foods like sugar, soda, and flour have caused our obesity problem. If you eat foods you were designed to eat, you won't be tempted to do any of the trendy cleanses because your fuel is already clean.

A WORD ABOUT SUGAR

When I was at the height of my sugar addiction, I attended the Shakespeare Festival in Ashland, Oregon. We stopped at a local chocolate store before the play. My sister, Gigi, and I each bought the same chocolate treat, and while we were eating it, she said, "It's too rich!" I thought to myself, *What is too rich? I don't know what that means. I have never had anything I thought was too rich!* Obviously, I had a serious problem! Today, items like that rich treat would have no appeal to me because they would be far too sweet.

All drugs of abuse—including nicotine, heroin, pornography, alcohol, and sugar—cause a particularly powerful surge of dopamine in the nucleus accumbens in your brain. Simply put, your brain sends out a feel-good response when you consume the addictive substance, later convinces you that you love it, and then that you need more. Every addictive pleasure eventually turns into some form of pain. In the short term, we come "down" from the pleasure, and perhaps feel shame or frustration with our lack of self-control. There is also the pain of the long-term effects, and every addiction has long-term effects. What are the long-term effects of sugar addiction? Refined sugar is the leading cause of obesity and contributes to heart disease, cancer, high cholesterol, arthritis, autoimmune diseases, depression, anxiety, Alzheimer's, and lack of vitality. Your brain is designed to protect you by giving the body what it wants. In the case of addiction, you must consciously override the signals.

Sugar addiction is rampant, and if you are addicted, then simply reducing sugar intake will not cure your addiction. Would you recommend to an alcoholic friend that they try "cutting back" on their alcohol consumption in order to cure their addiction? Would you suggest they only imbibe on special occasions, like birthday parties? What about the 80/20 rule, where they could say no 80% of the time, but the other 20% was okay? Of course, you would not suggest this to your friend. You know that, eventually, they will be drinking as usual. The same holds true for added sugar. If you choose the "cutting back" approach, it won't be long before you are owned by sugar again.

Giving up sugar does not mean you have to give up sweet. Since nature abhors a vacuum, think in terms of replacing those sugar-laden foods with something else that you love, but is healthier. Many of us are "hardwired" to desire sweet as a survival instinct. If that is you, then work with it instead of fighting it. You can have sweet and eat clean at the same time. When you practice replacing sugar-laden wrong-fuel foods with clean food, you will begin to prefer food that is less sweet. You will also become more aware of the natural flavors in real food.

When I was weaning myself off sugar, I would put a little honey on a spoonful of natural peanut butter and eat that when the sugar monster would chase me. My daughter said to me, "Mom! Do you know how many calories that is?" I knew, but my goal was to break my addiction, and I did whatever it took. Once I beat my sugar addiction, I no longer desired my peanut butter and honey treat. To help you get started, here is a list of favorite sugar hacks compiled from past clients:

- Plain Greek yogurt with a little honey and almonds (Kim)
- Fresh berries with Greek yogurt (Gigi)
- Banana with peanut butter (Beth)
- Dark chocolate, 70% cocoa or darker (Maynard)
- Frozen banana blended with cocoa powder (Chad)
- Chewing gum, preferably sweetened with xylitol (Mariam)
- Milkshake made with coconut milk and berries (Jeneen) ·
- Fruit (Alex)
- Cottage cheese (Meghan)
- Berries and whipped cream (FitMania favorite)
- Bonus tip: This is totally anecdotal evidence from personal experience and from experience working with FitMania clients, but raw honey doesn't keep the propensity for sugar up. If that helps, try a little, but don't go crazy!

My personal favorite is high-quality dark chocolate. The added sugar doesn't seem to perpetuate the addiction response, probably because of the nutrients and fat that occur naturally. I prefer chocolate with a minimum of 80% cocoa, but you might need to work up to that. Chocolate is also a great appetite suppressant too. If you are having afternoon cravings, try some chocolate first. There are a host of other benefits to chocolate, like lower blood pressure, antioxidants, improved skin, and better sex.

DEFENDING FRUIT

*"I don't think I'll ever grow old and say,
'What was I thinking eating all those fruits and vegetables?'"*

~ Nancy S. Mure ~

It is frustrating that there is a need to defend fruit, or any whole, unprocessed food. When the fitness noise becomes too overwhelming, and mixed messages are everywhere, I like to go back to basics. I go back to the way we were designed to eat, and how people have eaten for thousands of years. Humans have always eaten fruit. Fruit is the food group that requires the least amount of processing, and it is often naturally portion-controlled. A normal-sized apple, banana, pear, or orange is the perfect amount.

Fruit gets a bad rap because of its sugar content. However, fruit binds its sugar by trapping it amongst fibrous beta linkages, and therefore is digested more slowly than processed sugar or fruit juice. Fruit is also an important source of vitamins, minerals, and antioxidants, including very potent flavonoid compounds and anti-aging resveratrol found in the skin of grapes, dark chocolate, and blueberries. Because fruit is high in fiber, it aids in digestion. Fruit is visually appealing and tastes good, providing ample evidence we were meant to eat it.

THE PROBLEM WITH GRAINS

Here is a common conversation I have with people who are plateaued in their journey to be lean, but still eat pasta:

Me: You need to give up pasta. Try putting your favorite sauce on sautéed vegetables instead of pasta.

Them: But I love pasta!

Me: Imagine a plate of plain spaghetti with no sauce sitting in front of you, coagulating as it cools. What does it taste like?

Them: Not good.

Me: Then do you really love it, or could you be addicted to flour?

Vegetables have far more flavor than the cooling pasta, so why does the pasta have such pull? Flour is highly processed, so it shouldn't be surprising that bread and pasta are addictive. There is an increasing number of people with celiac disease, or who are intolerant or allergic to grains. Grains are often considered a whole food, but if you were lost and starving and came across a field of onions, turnips, zucchini, or potatoes, you could eat those foods immediately, even raw if necessary, and they would save your life. Those foods are whole foods. If you came across a field of wheat, what would you do? Wheat must be processed before you can consume it. It must be harvested, sifted, ground, mixed with other ingredients, and cooked before it could sustain your life.

People who are lean, and have difficulty getting enough calories, may need to eat whole grains. In my experience, grains, including oatmeal and rice, are weight gainers. If you do not need extra calories, get your carbohydrates from fruits and vegetables, including potatoes and sweet potatoes. They are better sources of minerals, vitamins, and other micronutrients.

EAT YOUR MACROS

There is always one fad or another that wants us to give up one of the macronutrients. Every diet plan, including keto, plant-based, Atkins, and South Beach, excludes sugar, flour, and processed foods. That is why they work. It's not because they cut a macronutrient or any whole foods. There are three macronutrients: protein, carbohydrates, and fats. We need all three, all of the time. We cannot be healthy without all three of these macronutrients, even briefly. They are needed for growth and development, sustaining circulation, and providing the brain with the energy it requires for cognitive functioning. We not only need all three macronutrients, but we need the many micronutrients they contain. All of these nutrients work synergistically to perform their functions and to keep our bodies healthy. Eat all three macronutrients at every meal. This method of portion size for each macronutrient is easy and prevents obsessing over calories:

- A portion of protein = the size of the palm of your hand.
- A portion of carbohydrate = the size of your clenched fist.
- A portion of fat = the size of your thumb if you pour it; or if you chew it, like nuts and avocado, what fits in your cupped palm.

WHEN TO EAT

Even when those Concrete Construction Supply trucks get the right fuel, they still need a steady flow of it. No engine is going to run well if it gets a blast of fuel and then nothing for long periods of time. Remember, you are an athlete who *eats and trains*. No true athlete will let themselves get too hungry. They know they need *real fuel real often* for peak performance. Eating five small meals a day, two-and-a-half to three hours apart, will keep you running evenly. More importantly, you will be much less interested in reaching for those wrong-fuel foods, if you are not hungry. I am a pretty disciplined eater, love the food I eat, and do not feel deprived at all. However, if I go too long without eating, then foods I would ordinarily never be interested in suddenly become very appealing, and it takes more willpower to leave them alone. Unfortunately, highly-processed and sugar-laden foods provide the quick energy our bodies crave when it has gone too long without food, and those are much more available than real food. The solution is to plan ahead. A good rule of thumb is to *know today what you will eat tomorrow.*

Many people have told me their problem is being emotional eaters. Most of us are, and it is normal. The solution is in *what to eat and when to eat it.* If you eat frequently, every two-and-a-half to three hours, you will not be hungry. If you are going much longer than three hours between meals, then real hunger may be the true source of emotional eating. When we are stressed, busy, or emotional, then we tend to not eat enough, and when we finally feel hungry, our primitive lizard brain wants something right now and something it can quickly turn into energy, such as highly processed junk food. Whether you are going too long between meals or you are truly eating emotionally, the solution is still to eat frequently. If you still find yourself driven to eat, for any reason, then do it. Just eat whole food such as some very dark chocolate and a few mixed nuts, which always works for me.

FOOD IS FUN

"If people have not been eating a thing for at least a hundred years, maybe you should wait a hundred years before you try it."

~ Summer Larson ~

It probably feels like this new lifestyle requires giving up a lot of foods. You may even wonder if there is anything you *can* eat. There are so many beautiful foods in the world: interesting fruits and vegetables, savory curries, juicy steaks, rich stews, fluffy omelets, soups, stir-fries, and fruity yogurts. Did you know there are fruits in this world you have never heard of? That was my experience when I saw all the various fruits for sale in the markets of Thailand. You are a grown-up, after all, and you can eat anything you choose. No one is forbidding you to eat anything. It is your choice. If your choice is to be healthy, then focus on all the great food in the world. Experiment, try new recipes, make it a quest to eat well, and love what you eat. Remember, *what you think about expands*. Once you dismiss the processed foods as an option, you will find the alternatives are unlimited. You are not embarking upon another restrictive program, but an adventurous journey!

If this way of eating is new to you, especially if you have done any dieting in the past, you might feel like you are eating too much. Remember, real food is far less calorie-dense than wrong-fuel food. You can eat more, feel full, and be consuming fewer calories. It is difficult to gain weight when you eat the right fuel. Be patient and trust this system.

Eating *real food real often* is a joyous way of life. You can be lean and healthy without ever being hungry and experiencing the irritability that follows. Isn't it a relief to know that food is a friend instead of an enemy? You will no longer need to use up your precious willpower to stay on some calorie-deficient diet. We are designed to eat. Whether a person desires to become leaner, or they are already lean and desire to gain more muscle, the solution is essentially the same: *Eat real food real often.*

A FEW RULES FOR GETTING THE RIGHT FUEL

- Only eat food that has a parent or grows from the ground.
- Before you reach for that cupcake, energy bar, or weight loss product, ask yourself if you have ever seen one of those hanging from a tree.
- We can have *sweet* without refined sugar. Eat foods that contain sugar naturally.

- Artificial sweeteners are just that—*artificial*. Your body was not designed to process them, and artificial sweeteners perpetuate our addiction to *sweet*.
- Meat, in proper portions, is part of a natural and healthy diet. Avoid meats that are cured with nitrites, nitrates, sugar, and other chemicals.
- You can have a healthy diet without meat, but it is more work because plant-based foods with protein typically have more carbohydrates than they do protein. You can end up with too many carbs before you get enough protein.
- Grains take a lot of processing before we can consume them, and many people find that grains cause bloating, digestion problems, inflammation, and have been linked to depression. Grains are usually lower in nutrition than other carbohydrates, like fruit. However, for people who need more calories, grains are helpful if they don't cause any other health concerns.
- Carefully read the food labels before you buy any packaged food. If you do not recognize every ingredient as a real and whole food, neither will your body.
- Eat food you love. If you don't like it, don't eat it. Do not be surprised if you find yourself liking things you haven't in the past.

TRAINING

"Lack of activity destroys the good condition of every human being, while movement and methodical physical exercise save it and preserve it."

~ Plato ~

When speaking to an organization for entrepreneurs about fitness, I asked the group to raise their hand if they thought that they would be more successful and would make more money if they were lean, healthy, and physically fit. I was gratified to see that every hand went up. I hadn't expected a unanimous response. We proceeded to have a discussion about why our level of fitness affects our financial bottom line in our various enterprises. Sometimes I feel like something I present is particularly powerful, and this was one of those times. I presented well, and the members of the group were highly invested in a lively and positive exchange of ideas. By the end, I knew I had them! Lives were going to change! Or were they? As I visited with members of the audience after the presentation, they lined up to give me excuses for not working out. After listening to the same excuses over and over, I realized nothing was going to change. These were thinkers, dreamers, and planners who think outside the box as a way of life, except when it comes to their own health. I was so disappointed I slipped out the door as soon as discreetly possible.

Everyone has their own story for not improving their fitness level, but in every case, it is a version of one or more of three excuses. Those three excuses are:

- Time
- Physical limitation or injury
- Money

TIME AS AN EXCUSE

"Those who think they have not time for bodily exercise will sooner or later have to find time for illness."

~ Edward Stanley ~

Have you noticed that some of the busiest people still find time for a daily workout? There are people who have jobs, are working on degrees, have families, and still never miss a workout. Do you wonder how they do it? These people have learned that training doesn't take time; it *gives* you time. It sounds counterintuitive, but here are a few reasons why:

- When we train our bodies, we are mentally sharper, physically stronger, and use our time more effectively.
- Training daily gives us a sense of control over our lives and our time.
- Being sick takes time. Training greatly improves the immune system and helps prevent everything from the common cold to cancer.
- One wise man said, "Do all that you can, to live as long as you can, to do all the good that you can." People who engage in physical fitness live longer, and that will give you more time.

The most effective fitness programs do not require you to spend long hours at the gym. Unless you are training for an event, or you are doing an activity for the love of it, you should not be spending more than forty-five minutes a day training. Once you incorporate fitness training into your daily routine as a way of life, and then miss a workout for some reason, you will find that you did not get any more done that day, and maybe less. At the end of the day, no one says, "I sure am glad I missed my workout today."

While having a full workload is often the excuse for not having time, being too busy taking care of other people to take care of one's self is also a common excuse. At first glance, it seems noble. However, like the instruction on airplanes to put your own oxygen mask on first before you help your child, taking care of yourself is an unselfish thing to do. When you take care of your essential physical, mental, and emotional needs first, your own cup is full, and you'll have more to give to others. And if you do not take care of yourself, eventually, someone else is going to have to take care of you. To require physical care from another person because you didn't take care for yourself is both selfish and unfair. It's like Jim Rohn said: "You take care of you for me, and I will take care of me for you."

PHYSICAL LIMITATIONS OR INJURY AS AN EXCUSE

"As long as the sufferer is in any way preoccupied with what his body is doing, the pain will continue."

~ Dr. John Sano ~

The truth *movement cures* can apply to so many kinds of pain and other limitations. My sister, Jamie, walked 560 miles in thirty-three days to complete the entire Camino de Santiago in Spain. She loved it so much that she did some other long walks. While she was walking the Coast-to-Coast in England, she hurt her leg and had continued issues with her calf muscle for many months. She tried a lot of therapies and therapists. She was told the muscle was forever torn, and her days of walking across countries were over. She had already paid for a walking trip across Scotland, so she went anyway. Instead of walking, she planned to take a bus to each stop along the way. On her first day, she decided to try walking before she took the bus. She did fine that day and ended up walking 188 miles in 14 days, across Scotland. Three months later, I was with her when she hiked ten days in the Alps and successfully completed the Tour du Mont Blanc.

Injuries are an inevitable part of life, but our bodies know how to heal themselves, and they do so pretty quickly. If you are waiting to heal from an injury, there is still plenty you can do. Think about how much of your body isn't injured and work those parts. A broken arm? You still have one arm, two legs, a body core, and a cardiovascular system you can work. Unless you are comatose or dead, you can always do something, and *you can always do more than you think you can.*

If you have chronic pain, the answer may be to move regardless of the pain. *Fearing activity because you are afraid of your pain may keep you more sidelined than the pain itself.* Pain may be very real and still have an emotional source. If you have chronic pain, then I would suggest you read *The Great Pain Deception* by Steven Ray

78

Ozanich, *Practicing the Power of Now*, by Eckhart Tolle, or any of the works by Dr. John Sano.

When you have physical issues, by all means, consider a doctor's opinion, but remember it is just an opinion, and the doctor does not care as much about your problems as you do. The doctor also does not know you as well as you know yourself. Take charge of your own health. Do your own research, seek many opinions, think logically and carefully about what is happening to you, and trust your own instincts.

MONEY AS AN EXCUSE

"Don't tell me where your priorities are. Show me where you spend your money, and I'll tell you what they are."

~ James W. Frick ~

At FitMania, money was often an excuse. Because our program was expensive, I would occasionally give a membership to a person who seemed sincere but truly lacked the money. I am not exaggerating when I tell you that 100% of the time, those people didn't make it through a month. They believed the money was the reason, but in the end, it was just an excuse. If someone wants something bad enough, there is always a way. There are expensive programs, but there are also a lot of ways to be fit that cost little or nothing at all. Gyms are cheaper now. Some online video programs are great, and there are some that are free. The information in this chapter will help you identify or develop an effective training program.

SHERRY STIRLING FERNANDEZ

FIT FOR SUCCESS

*"There's more to life than training,
but training is what puts more in your life."*

~ Brooks Kubik ~

So, we have time for fitness, but why is there a link between fitness and success? Here are just a few more benefits of training:

- Reduces stress
- Improves memory
- Improves brain function
- Develops self-discipline and persistence
- Improves immunity
- Improves pain tolerance
- Improves confidence
- Increases endorphins
- Increases testosterone levels in both men and women (this is a good thing)
- Improves sleep
- Increases energy
- Improves attitude
- Improves sex

CARDIOVASCULAR FITNESS

Are you one of those people who faithfully do long, steady cardio workouts? I see people at the gym running, cycling, stepping, etc., while reading a magazine, or plugged into a TV or cell phone—usually with a bored, joyless expression. If this is you, then the good news is you are way ahead of your friends, who are still in bed or sitting on the couch. A big pat on the back for self-discipline. The bad news is that daily steady-state cardio can cause your body to hit a plateau and slow your metabolism. When you put your body under prolonged stress, you start producing free-radicals, which damages your cells. Steady-state cardio (like jogging, spinning, or using the elliptical) increases the production of a stress hormone called cortisol. Cortisol causes your body to gain weight, especially around your stomach, and makes it even more difficult to burn off stubborn fat. This is why a person can train for, and run a marathon, without losing any body fat. There is also some evidence that running or cycling in place is confusing for our brain, because the body is moving fast, but the surroundings never change. There are better ways to be fit that are more fun and take less time.

The workout program at FitMania was a very intense forty-five minutes of simultaneous cardio and resistance training intervals. People would often ask me if they could also run or cycle on the days they worked out. The answer is a resounding YES! We are designed to get up in the morning, work hard physically all day long, go to bed, sleep hard, and get up and do it again the next day. A healthy metabolism is one where we *eat–move–eat–move–eat–move–eat–move* all day. Both eating and constant movement are keys to a healthy metabolism.

Even though moving all day is critical to being healthy, a good training program is also necessary, and it should include some intense cardiovascular activity. The first step to an effective cardio program is to put down the magazine and turn off the TV. Don't multitask when you work out. Some serious bodybuilders feel that even music is a distraction. Vince Gironda wouldn't allow music played at his legendary Vince's Gym in Southern California. The idea is to focus on the workout and appreciate what your body can do. So, you might try working out without music occasionally. We could all use a little time "unplugged" anyway. Do twenty minutes of *intense* intervals at least three times a week, using any activity that gets your heart rate up. How intense? On a ten-point scale where ten feels like a heart attack, aim for a 9.5 in each interval. If you should happen to hit a ten occasionally, that's okay. You won't actually have a heart attack.

An active lifestyle is a joyous way to live. If you love a certain sport, which gets your heart rate up, such as cycling, running, hiking, or swimming, then do those as long and often as you like, for the fun of it. Those activities vary your heart rate naturally enough, and are enjoyable enough, that they will only make you healthier. If you want to run a marathon, then absolutely do it, if for no other reason than to say you have done it. Just make sure some of your training involves intervals. Regardless of the sports you do, complete the twenty minutes of *intense* intervals three or more times a week. While you can do intervals on any cardio machine, being outdoors is always best. The interval is a nine or ten on a ten-point scale. The active rest is a five on the same one to ten scale. You will want to vary the actual length of both intervals and rests, every week or two. Here is a sample:

5-minute warm-up
1-minute sprint
2-minute active rest
1-minute sprint
2-minute active rest
1-minute sprint
2-minute active rest
1-minute sprint
2-minute active rest
1-minute sprint
2-minute active rest

That's it, twenty minutes! An hour on a treadmill will burn more calories, if you don't die of boredom, but when you are finished, so are the calorie-burning benefits. With interval training, your calorie and fat-burning benefits last up to forty-eight hours, plus it creates a hormone environment conducive to weight loss. It will also strengthen your cardiovascular system and give you an extra forty minutes a day (compared to the treadmill routine).

You may have heard the saying, "sitting is the new smoking," which is credited to Dr. James Levine. He's not the only one who believes that we are sitting ourselves to death. There's a growing body of research that supports his claim. Is sitting really the new smoking?

I don't know what that means exactly, but we aren't designed to sit much, and extended sitting is certainly hard on our health.

We always had exceptional results at FitMania, both in helping people get lean and strong, and in helping them make it a lifestyle. There was a small group of about ten people, mostly women, who never missed a workout. They trained hard and followed the food protocol but could not get the results most clients were getting. We checked and double-checked the food they were eating. We also sent them to specialists I trusted, to have their hormone levels evaluated. It wasn't until the last year of my time there that I fully realized the problem. All of these people had sedentary jobs, and other than their workouts, they moved very little during the day. To be healthy is to move, move, move, move!

MUSCLE

"I use my muscles as a conversation piece,
like someone walking a cheetah down 42nd Street."

~ Arnold Schwarzenegger ~

Strong is the new skinny was written on the back of the t-shirt of a pretty girl standing in line in front of me at Costco. I hope she is right. I would love to see trends for women move more toward strength and less emphasis on thin. Strength enhances your life, makes you more functionally fit, and capable. Skinny, if it comes from calorie restriction, makes you weaker and less capable. Thin is fine, but strong is infinitely more appealing and definitely sexier! Of course, there are people who are naturally thin, and, in that case, thin and strong is far better than just thin. The more muscle you have, the physically stronger you are, but the benefits don't stop with being physically strong. Here are a few benefits of increased muscle for both men and women:

- Protects from injury
- Provides bodily shape
- Improves immunity
- Improves sleep
- Increases metabolism
- Assists in the prevention and control of diabetes
- Protects bones from osteoporosis
- Assists in the control of hormones
- Assists in weight control
- Is attractive

Are you restricting calories? One of every four pounds you lose is probably muscle, unless you have a good muscle-building program. Even if you're not restricting calories, you still may be losing muscle. Adults lose one-fourth to one-half pound of muscle a year, unless they have a focused strength-building program. Tips on how to build muscle:

- Use body weight exercises as much as possible.
- Make sure your form is correct.
- Work as many muscle groups as possible at one time. You have hundreds of voluntary muscles. Try to hit them all!
- Look for muscle confusion by varying your routine of exercises, your repetitions, or the amount of weight you use.
- Be consistent. Work a muscle twice a week to make progress, and once a week to maintain it.
- Drink a lot of water, at least half your body weight in ounces per day (for example, if you weigh 180 pounds, then drink ninety ounces of water).
- Always eat before you train, and within thirty minutes after training.

Everyone can agree that muscular men are more attractive. If we didn't love muscular men, Arnold Schwarzenegger, Sylvester Stallone, and Duane "The Rock" Johnson would not have movie careers. What about women?

A woman, who trained at the same gym I did, was able to do a rare thing for a woman. While most women get tighter, leaner, and smaller with more muscle, she got big, defined muscles. Maybe that sounds like a bad thing to you, but it wasn't. She was gorgeous! Sometimes women will worry that they will "bulk up," but very few women can get bulky muscles. I think this fear is attached to women thinking we need to be a certain weight or size. If you have more muscle, you might weigh two to three pounds more, but not typically be larger, because muscle is more compact than fat. If you do happen to be one of those women who can get bigger muscles, don't hold back! Get all the muscle you can, and then send me a picture!

SLEEP

"Ours is a culture where we wear our ability to get by on very little sleep as a kind of badge of honor that symbolizes work ethic, or toughness, or some other virtue—but really, it's a total profound failure of priorities and of self-respect."

~ Maria Popova ~

There was a time in my life when my drive to accomplish caused me to resent the fact that I had to sleep. I had a friend who swore she only needed to sleep four hours a night. She would practice the piano, read, and accomplish projects while her family slept. I was jealous! I imagined what I could accomplish with three more hours in a day, and I wanted to sleep less too. I erroneously thought I could train myself to sleep less, so I started by cutting my sleep by fifteen minutes for two weeks. Then I cut out another fifteen minutes. I tried this a number of times, and every time I was about a week into my second cut, I noticed I was less productive, less creative, and more fractious. And I was tired! I now embrace the fact that I need at least eight hours of sleep every night, and eight-and-a-half are ideal for my best day. There may be some people who need less sleep than the rest of us, but my long-ago friend might not have been one of them after all. She began losing cognitive function early in life and had dementia-related issues before she was sixty. Sleep affects everything from your weight to your brain functions and your relationships. Here are a few tips on sleep:

- Train hard every day.
- Be as active as possible throughout the day.
- Meditate.
- Have a bedtime routine.
- Go to bed at the same time every night.
- Keep your bedroom dark—try blackout blinds.
- Avoid screen time before bed.
- Keep your bedroom free of TV, work projects, and hobbies. Bedrooms are for sleep and sex.

Bonus tip: A few years ago, Ken started snoring—and snoring loud! We have always loved sleeping wrapped up in each other, but it was starting to look like we might need separate bedrooms. We tried a lot of different things but without success. Eventually, we saw an ad for Smart Nora (SmartNora.com). We were skeptical but desperate. We bought the Smart Nora. It was totally non-intrusive, and it worked! Ken doesn't snore, so he feels more rested, and I sleep all night.

HORMONES

"Suspecting and knowing are not the same."

~ Rick Riordan ~

Our environment, our diet, and who knows what else, have caused a disruption in normal hormone function for both men and women. If you suspect you have a hormone issue, you are over forty-five, or simply curious, I suggest you find a good doctor with a legitimate medical degree who specializes in anti-aging and regenerative medicine. That doctor should make their diagnosis based on the results of a blood draw. You want a doctor who is looking for *optimal* levels of hormones for your gender rather than *normal levels for your age,* and if needed, will prescribe *bioidentical* hormones rather than synthetic. While they can prescribe hormones, *you will not get the expertise you need from your general practitioner or a gynecologist.*

Your doctor will also look at what nutritional supplements you need specifically, but generally, everyone needs a good multi-supplement, Vitamin D3 (which is a hormone), and vitamin C. Grocery store supplements are not ideal. I have found Life Extension (LifeExtension.com) to be an excellent source of high-quality supplements at a reasonable price, and they are an excellent company.

EVERYTHING AFFECTS EVERYTHING

"Everything affects everything else, and you have to understand that whole web of connections."

~ M. Mitchell Waldrop ~

For many years, I used an object lesson to demonstrate how affecting any one aspect of ourselves might affect others. I would cut circles and label each one with a major area of life impact: physical, emotional, mental, and spiritual. I would slightly overlap the circles, and then drive a push pin through the places they intersected, to make the point that affecting one of these selves would affect the other two.

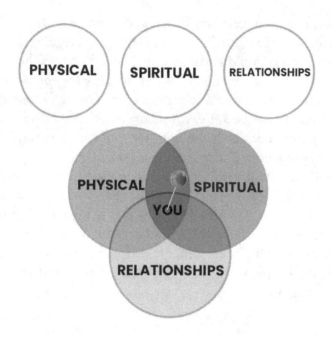

One day, I realized that I was not teaching the whole truth. In a moment of inspiration, I made eight circles by adding finances, business, lifestyle, and character. Then, instead of slightly overlapping the circles, I stacked them almost exactly on top of one another and pushed the tack right through the center. We are very complex creatures, and all aspects of ourselves are bundled together tightly. Everything that significantly impacts any part of us, affects all parts of us. To some degree or another, *everything affects everything.*

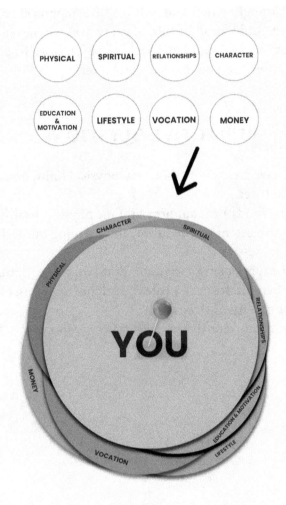

The essence of who we are is much more than our physical body. Perhaps that is why caring for our body might feel less important than our other enterprises. Some even consider it shallow to spend time and energy on our outward appearance. Indeed, it is possible to spend an inordinate amount of resources on the physical self. However, it is the body that thinks and works. Like any athlete on any playing field, the body is the instrument you use to be victorious. It is the tool you use to move toward your potential and the instrument through which you will feel the happiness to be found in the journey. And like all of Life Mastery, you will never see a time when you have arrived at the pinnacle of physical well-being. There are always new vistas, new ways to get better.

REFLECTIVE QUESTIONS

- Do I have any beliefs about my physical limitations that may not be true?
- Do the foods I eat support vibrant physical health?
- Am I consistently scheduling and carrying out well-planned training sessions?
- Am I experiencing fatigue, mood swings, or brain fog that may benefit from a professional hormone assessment or better quality of sleep?
- Does my current fitness level reflect who I am?

5

LIFE MASTERY AND THE SPIRITUAL SELF

"No matter how much I prove and prod,
I cannot quite believe in God;
But oh, I hope to God that He
Unswervingly believes in me."

~ E.Y. Harburg ~

The pursuit of spirituality is not a search for an opiate, as has been suggested. It is an uncomfortable and sometimes painful journey. Scott Peck noted how we make the journey harder for ourselves when he said, "Buddhists tend to forget the Buddha's suffering and Christians forget Christ's joy."[4] The road to spiritual enlightenment can bring you to your knees in despair, but also brings moments of joy that transcend all understanding. Remember, our purpose here is to be happy. So, it shouldn't surprise us that the Ultimate Father of the Universe would also want His children to be happy, would design them to be happy, and make all the information and tools available for our happiness. Like all good parents, He also allows us to struggle. I think spiritual evolution

---

[4] Scott Peck, *The Road Less Traveled, Timeless Edition* (New York: Simon and Schuster, 2003), 76.

is much like learning to understand great poetry—not easy, but a beautiful experience when we make the effort.

THIS TOO I BELIEVE

The sun was setting as I drove through a small rural community. On the road ahead of me, I saw a man walking with a woman who was holding the hand of a child. The scene looked so pleasant to me, but when I approached them, they vanished. My eyes had deceived me. That little family was a shadow in the evening light.

Our five known senses are critical to learning, and yet they are not always reliable. More than once, I have thought a bug was crawling on me and discovered it was a thread or loose strand of hair. Just yesterday, we made popcorn, and afterward, I would have sworn my house smelled like fresh-baked pastries. There are frequently times when someone says a certain thing, and then I discover what I heard wasn't what they said at all. Many times, I have thought through something carefully, been sure I have come to the right conclusion, and then realized I neglected a certain perspective. My intellect has also failed me more often than I would like to admit.

Neither our sense of reason, nor our senses, are wholly reliable. And yet, too often, we insist that unless we can hear, see, or feel a certain thing, we cannot believe in it. Some things descend to the core of our being and can be known with greater certainty than anything the physical world can teach us. Many of the most valuable things we know come from sources we cannot identify. For example, you know you love your children. You know this with certainty, and there is no source on Earth or in heaven that can make you doubt this knowledge. How do you know? Where is this feeling of love located? We say our heart is full of love, but the heart is a pump. The brain cannot feel love because the brain is a computer. The feeling of love does not center in our senses or our sense of reason, but there it is.

Similarly, but different, is the knowledge of spiritual things. This knowledge is aided by study, but it doesn't come from study. Miracles can be experienced through our senses and defined by our reason. Miracles can also affirm faith, but they cannot give us spiritual knowledge, any more than they can give us love. The knowledge of the mystical comes from somewhere inside us.

Even though knowledge of the mystical comes from the inside, it must be preceded by some tiny bit of faith or desire. It may seem convenient how the teachers of the various belief systems ask us to believe, at least a little, in order to develop our spiritual selves— needing faith as a grain of mustard seed, so to speak. Commenting on the need to believe first, Saint Anselm of Canterbury said, "Nor do I seek to understand that I may believe, but I believe that I may understand. For this too I believe, that unless I first believe, I shall not understand." It seems like a lot to ask at first, but it isn't much different than a scientist who has a hypothesis and goes about proving it is true. The search for truth in both cases is a great adventure with much to learn.

Terryl Givens wrote, "The quest for heaven has always been fraught with danger and ambiguity." Believing even enough to examine the issue is risky. Not only is there the fear of being duped, but there is also the fear of appearing gullible to the people who cannot fathom why you would take such a journey. The trick is to have such a love of truth, a love of adventure into the unknown, and to have such a burning desire for excellence in every area of life that you are willing to take the risks.

It has been said that happiness and peace are so close to being the same we cannot tell one from the other. Increased spirituality can bring peace as we come to realize there is order in the universe, and someone larger than ourselves is in charge. Approached with an open mind and an enthusiastic desire, the search for spiritual truth is a great adventure.

WHAT IS SACRED IS PERSONAL

"Sacredness inspires respect."

~ Toba Beta ~

When I was a teenager, my mother became temporarily involved in the church in which we were baptized. We had not participated in church up to that point, but when she started attending church, she pressured me to attend as well. As if that wasn't annoying enough, she also kept asking me if I was praying. I had adopted the practice of praying before bed during my precarious circumstances as an eight-year-old, but my spiritual feelings were very personal to me, and I was not about to discuss them on demand. What is sacred is personal. While I am open about my faith in God, and reference it frequently, I do not share all I know because those feelings and experiences are sacred to me.

Studies repeatedly show that people who have a rich spiritual life and a personal relationship with the Divine are happier than those who don't. Many more people than we might imagine practice a sincere faith and align themselves with some formal religious group. Even more are privately seeking answers to their questions. The goal of this chapter is not to tell you what to believe, but to show the value of spirituality, and offer some ideas on how to facilitate your own spiritual journey.

My husband's older sister, Judy, retired and bought a home near us. She and I began to spend a lot of time together, and we became good friends. Judy was a lifelong agnostic, maybe even an atheist. As far as I know, she never specified. One day she surprised me by asking what she might read that was spiritual but not tied to any one faith. I recommended she read *The Art of Happiness* by the Dalai Lama. She read it. She told me the book didn't particularly resonate with her, but it gave her some things to think about. Unfortunately, she contracted a rare and devastating disease a year later that quickly destroyed both her mind and body. I don't know where her spiritual journey took her. I wish I had asked her what had started her thinking about spiritual things. Perhaps she found herself thinking as Voltaire did when he said, "To believe in God is impossible; but not to believe is absurd." Skepticism is okay. In searching out truth of any kind, it might even be essential.

The world is full of mystery. Albert Camus wrote, "Truth is mysterious, elusive, always to be conquered. Liberty is dangerous, as hard to live with as it is elating. We must march toward these two goals, painfully but resolutely, certain in advance of our failings on so long a road." One of the things I love best about the spiritual journey is the unfolding of never-ending mysteries. It just takes a little curiosity to open up a whole new world of ideas. As you seek your own answers, do not be surprised if you end up with more questions. Like all of Life Mastery, it is the journey that enriches our lives. It is *personal progression toward an infinite potential that is the key to happiness.* The following sections are a few places to begin, or enhance, your own spirituality.

BE AWED

"Earth's crammed with heaven,
And every common bush afire with God;
And only he who sees takes off his shoes."

~ Elizabeth Barrett Browning ~

Martin Rees wrote, "We're not aware of the 'big picture' any more than a plankton whose universe was a liter of water would be aware of the world's topography and biosphere." The world is so full of mystery, and it isn't hard to be awed by its mysteries once we look outside of our own liter of water. I once heard a young woman speak with awe as she related some of the amazing things she witnessed during the year-and-a-half she spent in full-time service to other people. I no longer recall what those amazing wonders were, but I distinctly remember the light in her face and the sparkle in her eyes.

There was something she said that has stayed with me and that I occasionally repeat: "Be realistic. Expect a miracle." She had learned to see miracles, and she was awed by what she had experienced. The value of miracles is not that they reveal truth but that they are the impetus to seek truth.

There are wonders all around us if we look for them. It is awe-inspiring to watch the waves of the ocean come crashing in endlessly, one after another, then try to imagine the immensity of that same ocean and all the life contained therein. Or to see a redwood tree, a thousand years old, with its own ecosystem at the top. When the ancients of the Middle East sat outside their tents, in the desert and the darkness, did they look out into space and feel small in the vastness of both land and space?

It isn't just the big things that can awe us. My sister, Gigi, is a Master Instructor of SCUBA. She taught me to SCUBA dive decades ago and is still my favorite person to dive with. The underwater world is amazing but, just like the surface, we can become so accustomed to it that we cease to see it. Gigi has taught me that if I look at an ordinary piece of coral long enough, I may see something incredible, like minute shrimp and ornate nudibranchs. She has shown me eels, lobsters, rare fish, and sharks I would not have seen without her help. I occasionally practice this technique on the surface of the earth, looking at some small patch of nature. It is amazing what you can find in the tiniest bit of real estate if you watch it long enough.

Nature isn't the only source of awe. For some reason, I find our highways and waste disposal systems to be pinnacles of human achievement that are beyond comprehension. Of greater wonder are the beauty of cathedrals, the mysteries of the Mayan and Egyptian pyramids, and the architecture of beautiful buildings of the modern age. Great works of art, poetry, music, and literature can be especially inspiring achievements of humanity. However, humans have accomplished more astonishing feats than building highways and cathedrals. Every day across the world, people are performing great acts of courage in their ordinary lives, selfless acts that make the world a better place for someone else. We don't have to look far to find those miracles of love. Humans are truly extraordinary, and it is extraordinary how extraordinary the ordinary person is.

BE GRATEFUL

"The world is so full of a number of things,
I'm sure we should all be as happy as kings."

~ Robert Louis Stevenson ~

A traditional Islamic saying states, "The first who will be summoned to paradise are those who have praised God in every circumstance." The major emphasis of the Biblical Psalms is the expression of gratitude towards God. A fundamental focus of all the major religions of the world, including Hinduism, Buddhism, Christianity, Judaism, and Islam, is the importance of gratitude. Regardless of where a person is in their spiritual life, or what their belief system is, a good place to begin enlarging their spirituality is gratitude. The religious scholar Phillip Barlow writes:

> "My grateful mental state lets in a different view of reality than is otherwise possible...And when I am thus conscious of my life and the world as a gift, I am less preoccupied with self. My attention focuses elsewhere. I am more alert to other people's needs and virtues. I find my wonder awakened by just about everything: the engineering behind the physique of a cricket or a fly, for instance, or the beauty in even a pebble. In other words, when I am grateful, I tend toward a higher mental (and spiritual) state. I take things—people, order, air, roundness, everything—less for granted. Hence I notice things otherwise invisible to me. It is as if I have a sixth sense, taking in more context, more reality. If my temporary taste of gratitude becomes a disciplined habit, an ongoing attitude and state of mind, I am 'smarter,' more aware, than if this were not so. To the extent that I become a habitually

grateful person, I engage a different and richer reality than the 'me' who is less grateful."

In the last few years, there have been a lot of books published on the subject of gratitude, usually in the context of soothing one's own troubled soul. This is fine, but I sometimes think it feels a little more self-absorbed than grateful. Even though there are many benefits to being grateful, being grateful in order to attain the benefits misses the mark. I admire my good friend Jannica Johnson who has studied, practiced, and understands gratitude at a deeper level than anyone I know. I asked her to share some of her thoughts at a Life Mastery workshop, and we received fabulous feedback on her presentation. I asked her to put in writing her practical approach to gratitude:

One of my mentors says, "Until we know the WHY, the HOW doesn't matter." So let me you tell about WHY gratitude can change your life:

- What we appreciate APPRECIATES! We have so much good in our lives. Gratitude puts you in a position to GROW YOUR BLESSINGS because you are training your mind to focus on the abundance you already have.
- FOCUS on what you can control! There is much in your life that is not in your control, but your attitude and your focus is YOUR CHOICE. Charles Spurgeon wrote, "We are too prone to engrave our trials in MARBLE and write our blessings in SAND." Are you staring at your troubles or your triumphs? Do you see problems or possibilities? When you choose to count your blessings, you are choosing to fixate on abundance rather than scarcity or lack.
- Entitlement brings damage. Gratitude is a daily POSTURE and ATTITUDE of life...NO MATTER OUR CIRCUMSTANCES. Gratitude is developed in hardship and darkness and missed goals and disappointment and failures. Sometimes people hesitate to practice gratitude because they feel it lacks authenticity. They think it means things aren't

hard. But you can be honest about difficulty WHILE STILL being grateful for the good. Gratitude puts challenges into perspective. You don't have to change your life as much as you need to change your perspective.

- Gratitude improves relationships. It's hard to be hateful when you're grateful!

TRANSFORMATION does not come from more knowledge, it comes from ACTION. Here is the HOW:

- Gratitude Journal. I use my Jesus Journal to write five specific things down each morning before I read my Bible or do other journaling. It's a Daily Discipline. Notice the small things. Expressing thankfulness begins to flow naturally and without thought throughout each day!
- Look for some things you can be grateful for in someone who is tricky or difficult for you and tell them.
- Look for ways to be united to someone who is different or "other" than you.
- Move your gratitude out into the world. Write a letter of gratitude or a thank you note to someone who had an impact on you. Serve with your faith organization or a local charity as a way to give what you've been given.
- Give thanks in the midst of your pain and watch your perspective change.
- Give generously as an expression of gratitude.

READ SPIRITUAL TEXTS

"The nature of God's word is, that whosoever read it, or hear it reasoned and disputed before him, it will begin immediately to make him every day better and better, till he be grown into a perfect man."

~ William Tyndale ~

The world has known many great leaders who inspired their followers during their lifetimes and continue to inspire the world through the written word. It is nearly impossible to hear the teachings of Gautama Buddha, Socrates, Confucius, Mohammad, or Jesus of Nazareth and not feel inspired. Many of those great teachers did not write their own teachings. Gratefully, their followers have written their words, and they are now available to us as the basis of books like the Bible, the Torah, the Quran, and the Tao Te Ching. The Bible alone extends over six thousand years and contains a variety of authors, poetry, history, beautiful literature, and great stories. We are blessed to have access to them. These works are not easy reading, but worth the effort. We can also find truth, comfort, and spiritual enlightenment in the written works of other great thinkers of the past and present.

Inspired literature and great art can draw us toward the Divine. Spiritual maturity causes us to be more inclined to seek after "whatsoever things are true, whatsoever things are honest, whatsoever things are just, whatsoever things are pure, whatsoever things are lovely, whatsoever things are of good report; if there be any virtue, and if there be any praise" and to want to "think on these things" (Philippians 4:8 KJV). As I get older, I am more drawn to what is lovely, good, virtuous, and refined.

TRY MEDITATION

"Half an hour's meditation each day is essential, except when you are busy. Then a full hour is needed."

~ Saint Frances de Sales ~

It took a long time for me to try meditation. Because it was trendy in the "flower child" era of my young adulthood, meditation conjured up for me images of incense, long flowing robes, and wannabe gurus. And then, a few years ago, there was a period of time when it seemed, at every turn, I came across a very successful person issuing a testimonial for meditation as one of the major elements of their success. About the same time, I was learning some new concepts about chronic pain and the effects of meditation on chronic pain. I had also been having difficulty focusing my brain. I finally gave up my bias and began mindfulness meditation, and I have totally fallen in love with it. The Psalmist said, "Be still and know that I am God." Stillness alone is worth the effort meditation requires.

Meditation is both simple and hard. It is simple because all you need is a quiet place, and it requires little training. It is difficult because the mind is unruly. You will not need a guru to meditate with, but you might need a little help getting started. If meditation is new to you, I would highly recommend an app called Headspace (headspace.com). That is how I started, and I used the same method I learned from Headspace for a long time. I have now come full circle and do Transcendental Meditation, the fad of the hippies in my youth. You will need to find a teacher for a few sessions but no tie dye, incense, guru's, or flowing robes required. There is an extremely accomplished and well-known woman who claims to meditate three hours a day. I am sincerely impressed she does this, but it is an unrealistic expectation for most of us. I meditate twenty minutes a day, and it feels sufficient for me at this point. Start with a few minutes a day until you find what works for you. There are many proven benefits of meditation, but these are the benefits I have discovered:

101

- A quieter mind
- Peace in a troubled time
- Better concentration
- Elimination of chronic pain
- Better sleep

Meditation is a newer habit for me, but it has been a mind-expanding adventure, and I look forward to seeing where this particular journey will take me.

TRY PRAYER

*"Every evening, I turn my worries over to God.
He's going to be up all night anyway."*

~ Mary C. Crowley ~

While meditation and prayer are similar, they are not the same. I have no idea how I learned to pray. I started as a little girl who desperately needed my family restored and have prayed ever since. To have the best possible life, you must have the best possible days. Prayer improves my life, and I want the very best life possible. Every day is important to me. If prayer can improve my day, even an iota, then I must pray every day. However, my commitment to prayer is much deeper than that. William Nicholson expressed my feelings about prayer better than I ever could. He said, "I pray because I can't help myself. I pray because I'm helpless. I pray because the need flows out of me all the time—waking and sleeping. It doesn't change God—it changes me." Even with a lifetime of prayer behind me, I am keenly aware that gratitude is never as fervent as my pleading.

I seem to have come out of the womb knowing there is a God, so I haven't tried this, but it seems to me that if you want to know if a supreme being exists, then an obvious and risk-free approach would be to simply ask that being. Asking might also be a good approach if you'd like to better understand the nature of such a being.

TRY CHURCH

"What people don't realize is how much religion costs. They think faith is a big electric blanket, when of course, it is the cross. It is much harder to believe than not to believe. If you feel you can't believe, you must at least do this: keep an open mind. Keep it open toward faith, keep wanting it, keep asking for it, and leave the rest to God."

~ Flannery O'Connor ~

Are churches filled with hypocrites? Of course. Are leaders of churches fallible and imperfect? Yes. Are they occasionally evil? It happens. Evil people are typically good at finding ways to put on sheep's clothing, and they occasionally make their way into the sheepfold. If you look for fault in religious organizations, you will find it. Regardless of how inspired the organization is, it is facilitated by humans fraught with faults. Jeffery Holland said, "Imperfect people are all God has ever had to work with. This must be terribly frustrating to Him, but He deals with it." Since all of us fall short of perfection, to expect any organization, leader, or member to be perfect is, well, hypocritical. With all this imperfection at church, why try it? Here are a few reasons:

- It carves out a time specifically for spiritual growth. My dad used to say to me he could worship God going fishing just as well as in church. My reply was always, "You could, but you don't." There is something to be said about having a specific time to show up.
- It puts us in a place and frame of mind to be inspired.
- It gives us a community of other seekers of spiritual truth.

- To learn. You never know when you might hear a beautiful sermon or a comment from a fellow churchgoer that might change your life. I can think of several chance remarks made at church that altered my course.
- Simply for the experience. While I love my own church, I also have an interest in the religions of the world. The more I learn about various religions, the fewer differences I find between them.
- Increased opportunities to serve and to assist in another's spiritual journey.
- It is a place to practice loving other people. It is easier to be kind and loving when we are alone, but harder when required to mingle and serve with other people.

SERVE

"Hands that help are holier than lips that pray."

~ Sai Baba ~

Spirituality can be found in how we treat others. Small acts of service that bring comfort to another human won't make the headlines, but sincere, almost anonymous acts of service are the shortest road to holiness. I think that is what Terry Eagleton meant when he said, "Eternity lies not in a grain of sand but in a glass of water. The cosmos revolves on comforting the sick. When you act in this way, you are sharing in the love that built the stars."

It is interesting that evil can be done *en masse*. The Holocaust, the pogroms, the crusades, and genocides have caused untold suffering and the death of millions. Sometimes atrocities are committed in the name of religion and sometimes in opposition to a certain religion, but never for true religion's sake. When evil is carried out in the name of religion, you can be sure that the motivation is land, money, or power—not *pure religion*. "Pure religion…is this, to visit the fatherless and widows in their affliction" (James 1: 27) or in other words, to ease suffering, not to propagate it. Real religion is a way of life. In the words of Cardinal Emmanuel Suhard, "To be a witness does not consist in engaging in propaganda, nor even in stirring people up, but in being a living mystery. It means to live in such a way that one's life would not make sense if God did not exist." Interestingly enough, while evil can be brought to the masses in one fell swoop, it seems good can only be delivered one person at a time. When my own efforts to make a difference seem small and insignificant, I remember that Mother Teresa could only hold and comfort one wretched outcast at a time, and that Jesus healed the infirm one soul at a time.

REFLECTIVE QUESTIONS

- What do I consider sacred?
- Are there any spiritual practices that I've always wanted to adopt?
- What am I grateful for?
- What memories from my past triggered a sense of awe?
- Who needs my service?

6

LIFE MASTERY AND RELATIONSHIPS

PEOPLE NEED PEOPLE

"We want to live forever for the same reason that we want to live tomorrow. Why do you want to live tomorrow? It is because there is someone who loves you, and whom you want to see tomorrow, and be with, and love back."

~ Henry Drummond ~

In my hippy days, occasionally, one of my fellow drifters would declare they were going off alone so they could "get their head together" and "find themselves." I was suspicious back then of this concept but did not know how to express the error in this kind of thinking until I came across something by Thomas Szasz: "People often say this or that person has not yet found themselves. But the self is not something one finds. It is something one creates." It is true that each of us can benefit from regularly scheduled time alone. A short retreat is beneficial for reflection and goal setting. However, day-to-day growth requires interaction with people. It is easy for us to be tolerant, loving, kind, benevolent, and wise when we are alone at home. It is when we move through our day, bumping up against other people and their imperfections, that we see the extent of our own.

After having school-aged children for twenty-eight years, Andrew, the last of our six children, graduated from high school. About the same time, I found myself with fewer projects, and I was happily spending my days reading, cycling, gardening, and doing as I pleased. I was spending more time alone and loving it. It was during this time I added "I laugh easily and often" to my Daily Written Affirmations, but I was not making any progress on that one. One day I was chatting with a group of women when one of them made a chance remark. She said, "When you laugh with other people, it's healthy, but when you laugh alone, it's a sign you are crazy." My first thought was that she must have been "reading my mail." But I immediately realized she had no way of knowing I had been writing affirmations about laughing.

Once the shock wore off, I began to wonder how I could have missed something so obvious. If I want to laugh easily and often, I need people to laugh with. If I want to be more charitable, kind, empathetic, benevolent, loving, a better listener, to smile more, and nearly anything that is "virtuous, lovely, of good report, or praiseworthy," then I must have relationships with other people. In addition to the development of inner qualities, I have a mission *to assist others in their personal progress toward an infinite potential.* How can I live my Mission without association with other people? It is relationships that serve as a mirror showing us ways we need to change, and it is relationships that give us people to practice on. It is in relationships that we learn to be our best selves. We learn who we want to be in life and who we don't. You cannot become who you want to become without relationships. You will find joy as you experience deeper connections to the people you care about and enjoy the *happiness that comes from personal progress toward an infinite potential.* Here are some other benefits of having close personal relationships:

- We all need to love and be loved, and it is in relationships that we learn how to do that.

- Close relationships give us a safe harbor to share our most intimate thoughts, someone to count on and trust in times of need, and someone to rant to when it all seems too hard.
- Service is inherent in maintaining relationships; without relationships, we would not find the personal progression and happiness that comes through service.
- People who have strong relationships are more likely to live longer and healthier.
- The joy of human relationships makes life rich and worth living.

PEOPLE ARE FLAWED

"The art of being wise is the art of knowing what to overlook."

~ William James ~

There was a television show called *Father Knows Best* that was already old when I was a child. The show was about a family who had the ideal father. He would dish out the perfect amounts of wisdom, love, and kindly discipline. In reality, a perfect and all-knowing father would probably be annoying. My own father loved me, but he wasn't the guy from the TV shows I grew up with. His idea of being a good dad was to put a roof over our heads and food on the table. He might dispense a little discipline from time to time, but he wasn't home much. As an adult, my relationship with my dad consisted of going to lunch together every few months and trying to find enough in common to have a conversation. Even though he passed near my house on his way to and from his, he rarely stopped by, and he barely knew my younger children. I would wonder why he didn't take more interest in me and my life. My life was very busy, and when I was honest with myself, I would have to admit I really didn't want more from him. This, however, didn't stop me from criticizing his lack of attention. It was a dichotomy: I didn't want anything more from him, but at the same time felt perpetually critical he didn't do more.

For over thirty years, I have told the story of a day my dad fell short. I will tell it one more time here, but with some new insight and far less angst. It was Christmas Day in 1987. I was pregnant with our beautiful daughter, Merry Noelle, and she was quite overdue. I went into light labor at three o'clock Christmas morning. Merry was our fifth child, which meant we had four young children looking forward to seeing what Santa brought. We prepared so we could leave for the hospital at a moment's notice and then woke up our children. We had a pleasant Christmas morning with our kids, then got them ready for an afternoon of celebrating with extended family without us. My dad was married to his third wife at that time. Our tradition, in those days, was for my dad's kids and their families to meet at his house. I arranged for my sisters to care for my children once there, but my dad lived thirty minutes away, and I was running out of time.

All three of my sisters had children of their own, and I didn't want to impose on their Christmas, so I called my dad and asked if he would pick up my children. He declined and suggested I call my sisters instead. I was flabbergasted! I rarely asked him for anything, but I was in labor, and he wouldn't even pick up my kids? I have told that story as recently as last year, weeks before he died. It was at that telling that I thought of something I hadn't considered before. My dad was a heavy drinker in the evenings, and on a holiday, he started early. By the time I called him, he would have already settled in and had a few drinks. My dad wasn't above drinking and driving, but he would never drink and drive with children in the car. It seems so obvious now, that I cannot imagine why I hadn't thought of it before. In every relationship, we ascribe motive and assume intentions that are partly or wholly wrong. Even in this example, I can't be sure why my dad wouldn't pick my kids up on that Christmas day, but I am grateful he didn't.

Two of our granddaughters want to be geologists, and they both have rock polishers. The rock polishers work by tumbling the rocks together. They become smooth and shiny by rubbing the rough places off of each other. The process takes a lot longer than I thought. People also become better by bumping up against each other and polishing off the rough spots. This process, too, takes longer than

I wish it did. I work on myself all of the time, yet I am appalled at how far and how often I fall short. I continue to resolve to be better, make tiny steps forward, and hope those who love me won't give up on me. The poet Robert Frost wrote, "We love what we love for what it is," not for an ideal. In the end, it may actually be easier to love a flawed person rather than a perfect one. We can relate better!

WE DO NOT GET TO CHOOSE
HOW PEOPLE LOVE US

"The supreme happiness is the conviction that we are loved."

~ Victor Hugo ~

Shakespeare said, "The true course of love never did run smooth." Even the most healthy and loving relationships do not always run smoothly. People disappoint us, even when they love us with their whole souls. We also disappoint the people we love. It took a while, but I finally learned one of the best truths of my life. I learned that we do not get to choose how people love us. My dad might have left a few things undone—but let me tell you what he did. He expected me to ride a horse bareback before I rode with a saddle. He expected me to know how to check the oil in my car and change a tire before I could drive. He took his five kids camping, fishing, and trail riding.

In the early years of our marriage, when our income was so small that buying groceries was a desperate challenge, my dad showed up with a pickup bed overflowing with canned and bottled food that he had salvaged from the broken boxes of an Associated Foods truck wreck. On another occasion, he came by with an upright freezer. It was something we needed but couldn't afford. We paid cash for our cars in those days because that was the only way to buy a $300 car. Those cars only lasted a year or two, and then we needed another one. My dad always found us another old, cheap car that was big enough for our family.

My parents were married and divorced twice to each other, but he never criticized my mother. He never bothered me with his problems or involved me in anything that would distract me from my own concerns. He either helped, or he stayed out of the way. That's not a bad way to love someone. While I was wishing for a dad that loved me a certain way, he was loving me in the way he thought I needed and in the only way he knew how. No, we do not get to choose how someone loves us. In the process of understanding this truth, I also realized how important it was to my dad that his kids knew he loved us. In the last years of his life, I was able to reassure my dad I knew he loved me. What a tragedy it would have been if I had missed that opportunity.

Our parents, spouse, children, and friends will all love us in ways that work for them. Our angst will decrease, and our joy in personal relationships will increase when we recognize that people love us how they love us. Let the love in, instead of looking at how their love falls short.

We do not get to choose how people love us, and it is totally arrogant to try. I have always felt like our oldest daughter loved me loyally but would have liked a different kind of mother—one who would play more and was better at make-believe and dress up. I may not have been the mother she wanted, but she and I talked about this recently. She said I was the mother she *needed*. I think that is true. What we want from a relationship and what we need are often different.

For healthy relationships, we must not only love wholeheartedly, but we must learn how to recognize the love that others are expressing in their own way. Sadly, most of us are more inclined to hold a loved one emotionally hostage because they don't love us the way we would like to be loved.

Shortly after its publication, I read Gary Chapman's book *The Five Love Languages*. As I read the opening pages, it struck me how easily a person might be very loved and yet not feel loved at all. One spouse might be knocking themselves out serving the other because that is how they show love. Meanwhile, the other spouse is feeling unloved because to them, physical touch means love. Gift-giving and words of affirmation are my love languages, while giving quality time is not a strong suit for me. If I love someone and their love language is quality time, they may not feel loved by me unless they are wise enough to see how the gifts and the praise I give are demonstrations of my love. Of course, it would be wonderful if we could all show love in the way the beloved person needs it, and we should try, but as long as we continue to be mortal, we mostly fail at that. Instinctively, we love as we like to be loved. Of course, you can ask for what you need, and you may get it, but don't be surprised if it is not as satisfying as you hoped.

MANAGING TOXIC RELATIONSHIPS

"Toxic people attach themselves like cinder blocks tied to your ankles, and then invite you for a swim in their poisoned waters."

~ John Mark Green ~

A coaching client recently told me he didn't know what a toxic relationship was and didn't think he had any, and he probably doesn't. In my experience, however, almost everyone has a difficult, one-sided, or toxic relationship they are trying to manage. These are people in our lives who supposedly care about us, but don't mind hurting us if it suits their purposes. When we played games with my sister-in-law, she would say, "Right after me, you come first." She was absolutely not a toxic person, but her phrase is the perfect description of one: *right after me, you come first*. Here are a few signs of a toxic person:

- Passive-aggressive
- Bullying
- Controlling
- Demeaning
- Constant drama/ invents drama
- Lack of appropriate boundaries

- Persistent negativity
- Time/energy "vampire"
- Narcissistic

It took me over forty years with a toxic person in my life to finally learn how trying to "help" that person was a waste of time. These people do not see anything wrong with their behavior and have no interest in changing it. Even worse, their toxicity feeds on our efforts to help.

A relationship does not need to be toxic to be a relationship that is not worth your time. We have a limited amount of time to give to relationships. Save your time for the ones who you enjoy, that lift you up, bring value to your life, and whose lives you can positively influence in return. What do you do with the others? Try this exercise for managing relationships, especially the difficult ones:

- In the center of a full sheet of paper, draw a small circle large enough to write two to four words inside.
- Next, draw a larger circle around the small one, leaving enough room to write a few words between the two circles.
- Repeat this process at least three more times. It should look like a target.

Managing Toxic Relationships

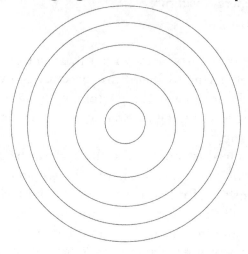

- In the center circle, write your name and the names of the people with who you know you can trust your heart and soul completely, and who are a positive influence in your life.
- Continue to place the names of all the people in your world that you want to, or have to, associate with according to the kind of impact they have on you. The following paragraphs explain how to place your names.

There are a lot of people in my world. My immediate family is over thirty, and my extended family is another thirty-plus. I have friends, church friends, and acquaintances. I have longtime friends and new friends. I have Facebook friends, and I have clients who I have grown to love, but my inner circle has me, God, and Ken. My kids are extremely loving and loyal to me, but it isn't their job to share my inner struggles, so they aren't there. My parents and siblings are not there, either. Some people do not have anyone close enough to include when they do this activity—it is possible that the only name you write in the circle is your own. That is okay. As you work on yourself, applying Life Mastery skills, the people you need will be drawn to you.

The second circle holds the names of those who are very important to you but do not belong in the first circle. They are the people who love you without judgment, in spite of your faults. My children are adults, and they go in this circle. I also have a few very good friends, who faithfully overlook my shortcomings. The second circle is not for anyone with who you do not feel completely safe, or anyone who tries to compete with you or looks for "chinks in your armor."

The third circle holds the names of friends and family members who just miss the second circle. The fourth includes those who barely miss the third. You continue this process, adding more circles as needed. When you have an unhealthy relationship or a person who disrupts your peace, brings drama, competes with you, or you don't trust entirely, but you can't bring yourself to completely let them go, move them outward to a larger circle. Then, only spend the time and energy on them that is appropriate for someone in a larger circle.

Managing Toxic Relationships

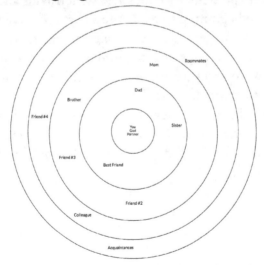

You can download the Toxic Relationship Worksheets at LifeMasteryInfo.com

When you move someone out a circle or two, do not tell them or discuss it with anyone. This change is about how you see them in your own heart and mind. There may be some people you move out again and again, until they are no longer in your life at all. If you have a hard time doing this with parents or siblings, just move them out gradually. In the long run, it will keep more peace in your relationship because you won't be storing pent-up frustrations and then exploding. This strategy allows you to keep people in your world without them hurting you or needing to have a "confronta-tion." You can spend less of your creative energy mentally wringing your hands over the toxic relationship.

This exercise is for your eyes only, and to be effective, you must be as objective as possible. *See your relationships as they are, not how you wish they would be.*

A system for managing relationships is especially helpful for teens and young adults, who are very attached to their people and can't imagine letting go of any of them. As we get older and a little less sentimental, we can deal with things a little more pragmatically. Young adults are particularly concerned with friends and family they love but are also beginning to realize how some of these relationships are unhealthy. As we get older, it is sometimes easier to see the value of completely jettisoning someone from our lives. It can still be con-fusing to know how to keep someone in our lives but not keep them close enough to cause damage. I taught a series about relationships to a group of adults who were mostly divorced and included this concept during the course. Some years later, I became friends with a woman who had attended that series. She told me this concept had changed her life.

MARRIAGE

"Almost no one is foolish enough to imagine that he automatically deserves great success in any field of activity; yet almost everyone believes that he automatically deserves success in marriage."

~ Sydney J. Harris ~

When I was growing up, marriage did not look appealing to me. This is probably because I had never seen a happy marriage. My mother was married five times and my father four times. When I was a girl, I did not dream of wedding dresses or who I might marry because I never planned on getting married. In spite of this, I fell in love with someone who loved me and loved my baby girl at least as much as he did me. I knew that for our relationship to progress, and for my baby girl to have stability, we needed to get married. Knowing that did not improve my less-than-romantic notion of marriage. I compared marriage to going to the dentist and thought, *There are some things you just have to do.* However, I decided if I was going to get married, I was going to have the most fantastic marriage ever, and I was willing to do whatever it took.

Finding good advice from anyone in my small and less-than-stellar circle of acquaintances was unlikely. I began reading books and articles on marriage and applying anything that felt right. Ken didn't read the books, but he liked me to share what I learned, and we attended a class on marriage together. It was during this period of time we began attending church, where we were learning, by both precept and example, ways to build a happy marriage. Obviously, we had some bumps along the way. You wouldn't find me credible if I said we didn't, but the bumps weren't anything serious. For forty-three years, we have had a romantic, sexy, companionable marriage that gets more romantic, sexy, and companionable every year. I can honestly say I have found, in marriage, the richest fulfillment of human existence. I believe, with all my heart, that happiness in marriage and parenthood can exceed a thousand times any other happiness.

Not everyone is married or has a life partner, so it may seem like I am spending an inordinate amount of time on this subject. There are three reasons why:

- The misery caused by an unhappy marriage makes the possibility of moving forward in the development of Life Mastery skills, and thus toward happiness, all but impossible.
- The happiness that comes from personal development and inching toward our potential is best when shared.
- Because my own marriage is successful, and because I have been teaching classes and lecturing on marriage for twenty years, I have some important insights on the subject.

I attended a lecture where a woman was presenting shared ideas on what men and women want in a marriage. It was so consistent with what I had discovered myself that I jotted down notes as fast as I could. When I began speaking and teaching on marriage, I meshed the things I had learned, by precept and practice, with the things I learned in that lecture. Willard F. Harley Jr.'s book *His Needs Her Needs* was already in print at that time, but I had not heard of it. When I finally came across the book, I was astounded at how close the things Harley taught were to what I was teaching. I believe discovering this book was a testimonial to the truth of what I teach, in a time when some of these concepts are less in vogue.

What follows here are my best tips on marriage. Like all of the principles in this book, it is the consistent application of these ideas that will make them effective. I am sharing general principles, which will not necessarily apply to every relationship. Do not dismiss an idea too quickly. Take time to think it through thoroughly.

WHAT WOMEN NEED IN MARRIAGE

Physical affection. My dad was never physically affectionate with us until we were well into our adult years. I considered my dad to be a strong person, and I subconsciously equated his lack of affection to being strong and independent. Once, a close friend who hugged me occasionally said to me, "You don't like it when I hug you, do you?" I assured her I did not. I was affectionate with my kids, my husband is an affectionate man, and I responded to his affection, but otherwise, I didn't even hug my sisters in those days. Somewhere in my early thirties, I realized that being affectionate was a strength, not a weakness, and I started hugging and touching people more. Now I hug anyone who looks like they wouldn't mind.

We know that babies need touch to thrive—they may even die without it. Adults may not die without physical touch, but we still need it to thrive emotionally. Being physically affectionate with your spouse is good for your relationship, and it shows others you value one another. It makes a woman feel secure and loved. It also assures your children, even adult children, that their parents' marriage is secure. Not everyone is naturally physically affectionate. If this is you, whether you are a man or a woman, think of it as a skill to be developed.

A man who will talk to her. We all want to be listened to, so I find it interesting that, in this case, a woman wants her partner to *talk* to her. Intimate conversation, for a woman, is a way to feel close to the man she loves. Both affection and conversation are important precursors to sex, but they also need to be part of a daily routine. Conversation will be especially important to women who do not have the opportunity for conversation in their workplace.

Absolute loyalty. Absolute loyalty means that, other than God Himself, the spouse comes first—before the children (ironically, this approach makes for happier children), work, sports, hobbies, friends, and parents. The spouse is only a priority to the extent you make them a priority in real time and with real effort. You may disagree in private, but in public, do not take a stand against one another. Do not say anything negative about your spouse to other people or share your marriage problems, unless it is with clergy or counselors. Do not complain about your spouse to your mother or your friend. You will get over the hurt and anger, but the person you shared with will always think a little less of your spouse. There is no room in an intimate relationship for other people. Online relationships and relationships at work that are anything more than professional rob intimacy that belongs to your life partner. Sexual infidelity shows a supreme lack of loyalty.

Financial security. Because women have a need for financial security, they may appear too materialistic. It is true that some women are greedy, materialistic, and money-grabbing, but that behavior should not be confused with normal inclinations toward financial security. Most women are not expecting riches, just safety. The need for financial security may be hardwired in women because they bring children into the world. Even if it is an unconscious feeling buried deep in our DNA, there are few things more instinctively dreadful to a woman than thinking she may not be able to feed her children. In this age of supposed equality, women are still more financially vulnerable than men, and especially if they have children. Perhaps that is why a woman has a hard time respecting a man who doesn't work, even if she makes good money herself.

Commitment to home and family. In our modern and enlightened age, men have taken on more responsibility in the home. Take a quick look around, and you can see how many women who work full time are still carrying most of the weight of family and home responsibilities. In matters of household responsibility, it may be because men abdicate, or because women want things a certain way and would rather do it themselves. If somebody isn't happy with the arrangement, then it needs to be worked out. In matters of leadership in a home where there are children, fathers need to be actively engaged in family life and demonstrate leadership.

WHAT MEN NEED IN MARRIAGE

Physical intimacy. I dislike jokes that stereotype men and women, especially husbands and wives. Too often, they hit at the heart of sacred or sensitive matters. It is never truer than on the subject of sex. In discussions with audiences on what men and women want in marriage, when I ask what women want most, it takes a while to get the right answer, and the answer is never accompanied by a snicker or a joke. When I ask what men want most, the answer comes up immediately, accompanied by laughter and a few smart remarks. When everyone settles down, I ask, "How did men get that way, wanting sex like they do?" Of course, the answer is that they were made that way. Why? One very important reason is that men feel love through sex. A man wants love as much as a woman does. For a man, sexual arousal is a prerequisite to being vulnerable enough to feel intense love. A woman needs love to open up to sex, and a man needs sex to open up to love. I love this quote from *Men Are from Mars, Women Are from Venus* by John Gray:

> "Men need sex to feel. For thousands of years, men adapted to their primary job as protector and provider by shutting down their sensitivities, emotions and feelings...For many men, other than hitting their finger with a hammer or watching a football game, sex is one of the only ways they can feel! It is definitely the way they can feel most intensely. When a man is aroused, he rediscovers the love hidden in his heart. Through sex, a man can feel, and through feelings, he can come back to his soul again... When a man touches the softness of a woman...he begins to feel his own inner link to experiencing pleasure and love. Through touching her soft femininity, he can reconnect with his own softness yet remain hard, focused and masculine...Many times after having sex with my wife, I realize that I had forgotten how beautiful the trees are in our neighborhood. I go outside and breathe the fresh air and feel alive again. In a sense, great sex helps me stop and smell the flowers. Although [a man] may not be aware of it, his persistent sexual longing is really his soul seeking wholeness."[5]

Just going through the motions is not enough. John Gray also wrote, "A man is empowered and nurtured most when he feels appreciated, accepted and trusted. When a woman is aroused, she is actually giving a man megadoses of what he needs most...A woman's

---

[5]   Scott Gray, *Men Are from Mars, Women Are from Venus* (New York: HaperCollins, 1992), 18, 28–29.

sexual responsiveness is the most powerful way he can hear he is loved" (Gray, 1992, p. 19).

At a bridal shower for my niece, each of us was asked to share our best marital advice. Our daughter Katie, who had been married for twelve years at that time, gave some excellent advice on handling disagreements: "Sometimes just having sex is more effective than hashing out your issues because most of your issues are not real problems anyway."

While affection is important in marriage, most acts of affection are common in other relationships. We kiss our mothers, hold the hand of a child, and we hug friends. Only sex is reserved for this one most important and unique relationship.

An available wife. Relationships usually die because of a slow leak rather than a major blowout. Even if a major event seems to be the issue, if we look further, we see the relationship was not being nourished. What feeds a relationship? Time. Time together was what made the relationship blossom in the first place, and it is time together that will keep it healthy and make it grow now.

- Spend a few minutes every day talking, but not about kids, bills, or household issues. Talk about the kinds of things you talked about when you first started dating. Stephen R. Covey had a big family and a lot going on. He took his wife out on a motorcycle ride every day so they could get a few minutes together to talk.
- Go on a weekly date away from the house. Why? Because the house is a source of "to-do's." It is brimming with things that need fixing or cleaning. You can't really get away when you are noticing dust bunnies and what needs painting. Ken and I have always done this, even with little money and a house full of kids. Our fourth baby, Christopher, weighed just short of ten pounds when he was born, so when I was pregnant, I was as big as a barn! Ken and I, with my big belly, were quite a sight as we rode an old motorcycle, because fuel was cheap, on our weekly date. We rode to Burger King because we received a free order of fries when we bought two

hamburgers. Going out with other people is fun, but it isn't a date. Going to the movies doesn't make a good date unless you go to dinner first so you can have a chance to talk.

- Get away for a few days. I have no idea how we managed it in the early days, and it was rarer then, but we found ways to get away at least overnight. This gives you a chance to get away from your responsibilities and just be two lovers, locked away from the world.

Spending time together is fun, and it builds the relationship in the moment. It also builds memories, like tiny threads, which bind you together. If you have enough of these tiny threads, it will build a bond that cannot be broken.

Praise and admiration. Everyone likes a compliment, and what woman doesn't want to hear she is pretty? However, praise is different. Men need praise for who they are and what they do, for their strength, ability to lead their family, fix things, making love to their wife, and anything that makes them feel manly. Our society is hard on men. If you have men in your life that you love, do them a favor and help them feel like men.

An attractive wife. Good men are not looking for their partner to look like a supermodel, and men typically give a partner far more credit for her looks than she might give herself. What men want is a mate who takes care of herself, is pleasant to spend time with, and who he can be proud of in public.

Domestic support. Everyone wants to have a tranquil home at the end of a hard day, but it appears to be an emotional need for men. This is not a license to leave the chores to his wife. However, limiting those chores so there is time in the evening to relax together will serve everyone.

TWO HALVES OF A WHOLE

*"Marriage: that I call the will of two to create the one
who is more than those who created it."*

~ Friedrich Nietzsche ~

In the window of a store that sold clothing for children, I saw a t-shirt that said, "The future is female." It's catchy, but it's false. Men and women need each other to have any kind of meaningful future, both as partners and as a society. If you look closely at the list of things women want and the list of things men want, they look less diametrically opposed and more like two sides of the same coin:

Affection + Sex
Conversation + An available wife
Praise + Loyalty
Financial security + An attractive wife
Leadership in the home + Domestic support

Men and women are two parts of a whole, and when we disparage one, we damage both. We need less posturing and bickering between men and women, both at home and in public. Instead, we need more anxious concern for the happiness of one another, both at home and in public. One of the greatest things a man can do for his wife is to make her feel like a woman, and one of the greatest things a woman can do for her husband is to make him feel like a man. That is not demeaning to one or the other. It isn't sacrificing your dignity to meet your partner's needs. This is love.

SOLVING PROBLEMS IN MARRIAGE

Electricity might have been free for all our lack of concern in using it when I was growing up. We turned a light on when we wanted the room lighter and turned it off when we wanted it dark. Ken was raised in a very frugal family, and they were adamant about turning lights off when you leave a room. It was a perfect setup for friction in a young couple's new marriage. Ken wanted me to turn the lights off when I left a room, and I tried a little. It just didn't feel important enough for me to make the effort to change my habits. Ken would show his frustration by stomping around the house and turning the lights off. One day I realized he still turned the lights off, but without stomping or other signs of annoyance. When I asked him about it, his answer was humbling and taught me a valuable lesson. He said, "I realized you were more important to me than having the lights off."

Every marriage has problems. There are problems like abuse, narcissism, infidelity, or porn addiction that can be deal-breakers in a marriage. Certainly, if children are at risk by one parent, they become a top priority by the other. Short of those extremes, the rest are ordinary day-to-day problems, and the nature of those problems is not important to the success of the marriage, at least not in and of themselves. However, *how we solve the problems is critical.* Drs. John Gottman and Julie Gottman have researched marriage for forty years and are founders of the Gottman Institute. I recommend any of their books. In Dr. John Gottman's book *What Makes Love Last?* he discusses four negative modes of communication he calls the Four Horsemen of the Apocalypse.

- Criticism: The least damaging but may cause the most lasting damage.
- Contempt: The most likely to lead to a failed marriage.
- Defensiveness: Forms of defensiveness are righteous indignation, counterattack, acting like an innocent victim. Defensiveness adds to the tension and lacks accountability.
- Stonewalling: Acts like a stone wall, ignoring. Stonewalling is the "cold shoulder" treatment and is hostile, childish, and cruel.

Any of these approaches will leave one partner with unresolved feelings and damages the relationship. On the other hand, when we solve problems with sincere consideration for each other; and with unity, love, and faith in each other, those trials will strengthen the marriage.

CHILDREN

"You may have tangible wealth untold;
Caskets of jewels and coffers of gold.
Richer than me you can never be-
I had a mother who read to me."

~ Strickland Gillilan ~

If you are looking for the perfect recipe for raising kids, I can't help you. Even though my kids came from the same gene pool and background, I never found a formula for raising kids which worked for all of them. There are wonderful books on parenting, and I certainly recommend reading as many as you can. As I mentioned at the beginning of Part II, these chapters are intended to give you ideas for setting goals. You can't raise a large family without learning a few things.

When you raise kids, you are going to have a few regrets. It is inherent to parenthood. No loving parent completely escapes a little remorse about lost opportunities. If I were to choose one thing to do differently, I would have spent more time with my kids, just enjoying being with them. We spent a lot of time with our children. We chose to spend our money on adventures rather than things. When money was tighter, our travel adventures were camping and trips to see family. As they got older, we took them on more exotic trips. Sundays were a family day. We cooked a nice meal together, went for a walk, played games, and had a short spiritual lesson. On Monday nights, we did an activity together. They loved picnics, hikes, and bowling; we still talk about the sock wars we had. We did all of this, and much more, and I still wish I had spent more time with them.

In the early days of parenting my own children, I read a book written to fathers. The author had some teenage sons, and he was explaining in his book how hard it is to get teenagers to share what is on their minds. He realized his boys were more open to having conversations about important things if he spent some time with them first. The boys loved basketball, so this good father spent a lot of time playing basketball with those kids. Connecting with kids requires an investment of time.

From the time my first child was born until the last one graduated from high school, I spent thirty-three years raising kids. This is far longer than average. Even so, it will still only amount to a third of my life. That leaves two-thirds of my life without children in my home. When they were young, I longed to travel, but until I was forty, we only took inexpensive trips that were close to home. Since then, I have been to all seven continents, forty countries, all fifty states, and I have big plans for the future. I love my life, and I wouldn't trade it, but hardly a day goes by that my heart doesn't long for my little children. If I had one wish, it would be to go back and spend an hour with each of them when they were still mine. Here are a few suggestions on ways to spend time with your children:

- Read to them.
- Eat meals together.
- Have family nights.
- Take family vacations.
- Take children individually on a "date."
- Play games as a family.
- Tell them about your favorite memories of them.
- Make your home welcoming to their friends.
- Hug them as much as they will let you.

BE NICE

"People are often unreasonable and self-centered.
Forgive them anyway.
If you are kind, people may accuse you of having ulterior motives.
Be kind anyway.
If you are honest, people may cheat you.
Be honest anyway.
If you find happiness, people may be jealous.
Be happy anyway.
The good you do today may be forgotten tomorrow.
Do good anyway.
For you see, in the end, it is between you and God.
It is never between you and them anyway."

~ Mother Teresa ~

People are rude, demanding, difficult, selfish, unresponsive, and self-centered. That is one viewpoint, and it is valid as far as it goes. It is also true that everyone struggles, and much of the bad behavior we see comes from fear or is a reflection of their suffering. Over my years of coaching, I had people in my office sharing struggles I had previously not known about, or didn't know their extent. When I better understood the extent of their problems and their pain, I wondered how they even got up in the morning. Yet, to watch them live their lives, you would never know. Since we do not know for sure the extent of another's pain, it is best to handle difficult situations with kindness.

One of my personal weaknesses is that I err too often on the side of *justice* rather than *mercy*. When someone's behavior isn't what I think it ought to be, my first inclination is to straighten them out. Because of my bias toward *justice,* I occasionally struggle to find a more merciful way of handling a problem. This was the case when I was a member of a gym where the free weights area was small, and I was frequently in close quarters with some men who trained at the same time. My problem wasn't sharing the space. If you spend a lot of time in a gym, you learn how to do that effectively. My problem was the language they used and other more minor gym etiquette violations, like excessive grunting, groaning, and dropping weights. The longer this went on, the more my feelings of frustration escalated. I began envisioning ways to tell those clods off, but I didn't want to make things awkward in a space I loved. Finally, I asked a friend of mine who had an outstanding ability to handle problems in peaceable ways what she would do. She suggested pulling the two main offenders aside, *spend some time* chatting, build a little bit of rapport, and then explain my problem. The solution seemed so obvious, once she said it, that I was embarrassed I had to ask. It is also embarrassing to admit it has only been recently that I added *I am kind* to my affirmations. While it took me far too long to add that affirmation, I have reflected frequently over this phrase from Wayne Dyer: "When given the choice between being right or being kind, choose kind."

CHOOSE CAREFULLY

"Tell me with whom you consort, and I will tell you who you are;
if I know how you spend your time, then I know
what might become of you."

~ Johann Wolfgang von Goethe ~

Have you ever avoided someone because their negativity dragged your own attitude down? Have you noticed you are happier when you are around happy people? We should be nice to everyone, even if we can't quite seem to love them. That doesn't mean you need to spend time with everyone who demands your attention. Who you spend your time with might be more critical than you think. Do as Wilfred Peterson suggests: "Walk with the dreamers, the believers, the courageous, the cheerful, the planners, the doers, the successful people with their heads in the clouds and their feet on the ground."

Did you know that entrepreneur means risk-taker? Entrepreneurs are big thinkers and big dreamers. I coach a lot of entrepreneurs, which is not coincidental. They have dreams, and they have ideas. Seeking out a coach to help them facilitate those dreams is a logical course of action.

Jim Rohn was fond of repeating the idea that we are the sum of the five people we spend the most time with. Big-idea people love to talk with other like-minded people. They want to talk about and listen to big things and big ideas. Ken and I host what we call BIG THINKERS dinners. Some of these dinners are small groups that can sit around a table and talk, and some are large groups where they mingle. The only criteria to be invited is to be a person with big ideas and a positive outlook on life. Typically, no one knows everyone there, and we don't do icebreakers. We also do not serve alcohol. I simply introduce everyone to the group, giving a tiny hint about what they do, and then sit back and watch them talk. The conversation is animated, they stay a long time, and they go away with new ideas and new contacts. Big thinkers and entrepreneurs need conversation with people who love to talk about ideas, but they are difficult to find.

When I need inspiration, want to learn at the feet of another person, talk about new ideas, or have a conversation that renews my passion, I seek out time with friends and associates who are standing on higher ground than I am. Cast about for these people and build relationships with them. They will become part of the team of people who will inspire you to make your dreams come true. This is why Confucius said, "If you are the smartest person in the room, then you are in the wrong room."

LISTEN

"People don't listen to understand. They listen to reply. The collective monologue is everyone talking and no one listening."

~ Stephen Covey ~

There is an insightful story about the two great prime ministers of England, William Gladstone and Benjamin Disraeli. I like this version told by Robert Mening:

"Benjamin Disraeli and William Gladstone were competing for the position of the prime minister of the United Kingdom. These two leaders went down in history, but with very contrasting personalities. Not surprisingly to the people of that time, Benjamin Disraeli won the election. Now, William Gladstone was a very clever and witty person. He was brilliant, obviously so, and he knew pretty much everything. Based on his wit and experience, he had what it took to win the election. What made the difference, however, was summed up by a woman who had dinner with both Disraeli and Gladstone a week before the election. The lady both men dined with was Jennie Jerome, Winston Churchill's mother. When a journalist asked Jerome what her impression of the two men was, she responded: 'When I left the dining room after sitting next to Gladstone, I thought he was the cleverest man in England. But when I sat next to Disraeli, I left feeling that I was the cleverest woman in England.'"

Everybody wants to tell their story. As harsh as it sounds, no one wants to listen to you talk about yourself. Well, hardly anybody. Pay attention when you chat at a cocktail party, run into a friend at Costco, or visit with the bank teller. Ask them a few sincere questions about their life, work, family, and what they are doing in life. Just get them talking a little without inserting your own story. Then notice if they get around to asking about you. When you realize most people don't care about your story, and they just want to talk, it frees you up to give the gift of listening. That might turn out to be a gift you give yourself as well. Jon Call shares this insight in *Tribe of Mentors* by Tim Ferris:

"I have gotten better at telling my brain 'no' when it wants to relate to conversation with a 'bigger' story. What I mean is, somebody might be telling me a story about an experience they had, while I have related a story that sounds even bigger or more dramatic than theirs. Rather than jump in with mine, I'll just let that desire go and ask them more questions about their experience. What I have discovered is incredible: the loss of the opportunity to possibly impress someone is far outweighed by what I learn when I ask more questions. There is always something more to their story that will amaze you. Don't expect that what they start with is as exciting as it will get. Ask and encourage them to say more!"

Even if the conversation isn't exciting, if you sincerely show an interest in the other person, you will leave the interaction feeling better about yourself than if you had spent the time impressing the other person.

THE POWER OF WORDS

"Words are singularly the most powerful force available to humanity. We can choose to use this force constructively with words of encouragement, or destructively using words of despair. Words have energy and power with the ability to help, to heal, to hinder, to hurt, to harm, to humiliate and to humble."

~ Yehuda Berg ~

What if everything we say matters? If you interpret the Judeo-Christian texts strictly, then God created the world with words: "And God said, Let there be light...And God said, Let there be a firmament...And God said, Let the waters be gathered...And God said, Let the earth bring forth grass...And God said, Let the waters bring forth abundantly...And God said, Let us make man in our image" (Genesis 1:26. KJV). Might it be possible that every word we speak is creating or destroying?

People are certainly shaped by words. A Japanese college student had a dream to attend a certain university in the United States. Her experience did not match her expectations. Her English wasn't as good as she had hoped, which made both school and social life difficult. To make matters worse, one of her classes was a volleyball class, and she had no aptitude for volleyball. One day in the class, it was her turn to serve the ball, and she had yet to do it successfully. Just as she was ready to serve the ball, a young man in her class said, "Come on, you can do it!" and she did. From that point forward, when things were hard, she would hear that young man's voice saying, "Come on, you can do it!" She told the story after she returned to Japan, and she said that encouraging phrase, "Come on, you can do it!" was a phrase she still repeated in her mind when she faced a challenge.

Another woman, whose name I do not even know, was one who helped shape who I have become. I doubt she thought she had such power. I was on the staff of a personal development workshop. This woman was one of the participants. She was an attractive middle-aged woman with rheumatoid arthritis. The pain she had endured for years showed in her eyes. She used two crutches to get around, and it looked like every step was a painful effort. Our breaks at the workshops were short, and the restrooms were very crowded. At one break, this woman bravely worked her way through the crowded restroom to find me. She said she wanted me to know how much she admired my energy and zest for life. I believed her! No one would work that hard to pay a compliment to someone unless they meant it. For years, if I felt myself dragging through a day, or through a chore, or through a workout, I would remember her words, pick up the pace, and adjust my attitude. I became more of what she admired in me, because of a simple compliment.

My husband has impacted my physical appearance by his words. Throughout my adult life, I have had multiple people tell me I was getting more attractive with age. If that is true, then I will credit my husband. He always refers to me as his beautiful wife to other people. He also tells me consistently and sincerely how beautiful and sexy I am. He makes me *feel* beautiful, and if there is a recipe for *looking* beautiful, it is *feeling* beautiful. Can you imagine how fabulous it is to feel beautiful and sexy at age 65? That is the gift my husband gives to me through his words.

Of course, this power of words cuts both ways. In another of Gary Chapman's books, *Love as a Way of Life,* he uses the metaphor for words as either "bullets or seeds." We all know people who have been hurt by the words of others and suffer almost irreparable damage as a result. Maybe this is why the New Testament warns, "But I say unto you, That every idle word that men shall speak, they shall give an account of in the day of judgement" (Matt 12:36). These words from C.S. Lewis have given me pause over the years:

> "The load, or weight, or burden of my neighbor's glory should be laid on my back, a load so heavy that only humility can carry it, and the backs of the proud will be broken. It is a serious thing to live in a society of possible gods and goddesses, to remember that the dullest and most uninteresting person you can talk to may one day be a creature which, if you saw it now, you would be strongly tempted to worship, or else a horror and a corruption such as you now meet, if at all, only in a nightmare. All day long we are, in some degree, helping each other to one or other of these destinations. It is in the light of these overwhelming possibilities, it is with the awe and the circumspection proper to them, that we should conduct all our dealings with one another, all friendships, all loves, all play, all politics. There are no ordinary people. You have never met a mere mortal. Nations, cultures, arts, civilizations—these are mortal, and their life is to ours as the life of a gnat. But it is immortals whom we joke with, work with, marry, snub, and exploit—immortal horrors or everlasting splendours."

Imagine what would happen if you and I were to leave every person with whom we interact better than we found them. Think of the dent that would put in the universe!

QUESTIONS FOR REFLECTION

- Do I truly listen when others talk?
- Are there any relationships in my life that I would like to be stronger and more intimate?
- Are there any relationships in my life that are toxic?
- Is there anyone I need to forgive?
- Do I create opportunities to openly and lovingly communicate with the people closest to me?

7

LIFE MASTERY IN EDUCATION AND MOTIVATION

BECOMING EDUCATED

"Formal education will make you a living;
self-education will make you a fortune."

~ Jim Rohn ~

Too many people leave education behind when they leave college. A four-year degree is useful, and young people should get one, but at this point in the world, a four-year degree only proves you can get a degree. Having a degree is good, and it says a lot about a person, but unless that person is getting advanced degrees, it will not provide much financial success. In *Think and Grow Rich* (the original 1937 unedited edition), Napolean Hill wrote, "[Someone said] 'knowledge is power.' It is nothing of the sort! Knowledge is only potential power. It becomes power only when, and if, it is organized into definite plans of action, and directed to a definite end."

The years Ken and I might have spent preparing for life, we spent partying instead. However, when we decided to get married, we left that lifestyle and those friends behind. We quickly made new friends with other couples, which was great, but it was also intimidating because it seemed everyone else had college educations. I assumed everyone knew more than I did, and they might have, but I was developing a daily habit of self-education, not to ease my self-doubt, but because there was so much I wanted to know. Gradually, I became more confident as I realized I did not need a college degree to be well-educated. A friend with a master's degree would frequently ask me how to punctuate sentences or other basic information. One day I asked her how she could have so much education and lack basic knowledge of fundamental things. She said, "I didn't get an education, I learned how to work the system."

College educations have become much more accessible in our modern age, but learning for its own sake has almost become a lost discipline in our school system. The goal of grade school is to prepare the student for junior high, which prepares the student for high school. A good high school prepares the student to get into a good university in order to get a good job with retirement benefits. Does that ultimately make the goal of grade school retirement?

While listening to a lecture, I became intrigued by a culture that preceded the classical Greek culture by a few hundred years. They had been an educated society with a written government and citizens who could read and write, but the whole society descended into illiteracy. To have a whole nation become illiterate is hardly unique in the history of the world, but this story started me thinking about how knowledge can be lost—not just by nations but by individuals. We can easily lose what we know if our knowledge is not continually used, built upon, and refined. Like the pursuit of a lean and strong body, knowledge must be a consistent and relentless journey. If we ease up, we lose ground. Remember, there is no status quo in the universe, and *personal progression toward an infinite potential is the key to happiness.*

A woman who was highly educated in the field of anthropology took a class I was teaching. She enjoyed the class and had high praise for my ability as a teacher. Eventually, she asked what my degree was in, and I had to tell her I didn't have one. There is an excellent university in my city where I have taken classes over the years and could have returned to graduate, once my kids were raised. I had always assumed I would get that degree, but when the time came to get serious about it, I realized the actual degree didn't mean much to me. What I really wanted was knowledge, and a university education was too slow. There are many avenues to education, and self-education is one of them. I designed my own course of study using some of the fabulous programs available. My best discovery was the Great Courses (thegreatcourses.com). It is a series of university-level audio and visual courses, produced and distributed by the Teaching Company, and they are outstanding. Other self-directed learning options include:

- Auditing college courses
- Online courses
- Reading books and periodicals
- Video programs
- Museums
- Cultural events

In order to take our then-fifteen-year-old grandson, Brady, with us when we hiked Tour du Mont Blanc, he had to miss the first two weeks of school. We immediately discovered Brady was easily a better navigator than the four adults. He led us through the countries of France, Italy, and Switzerland by foot, using the same route many Jews took to escape occupied France during World War II. Those Jewish refugees, we learned, were most frequently led through the mountains to safety by teenage boys like Brady. Would he have learned more had he been in school those two weeks? There are more ways to obtain an education than reading or taking courses. Learning through experience can include the following:

- Traveling
- Meeting new people
- Exploring nature
- Joining think tank or mastermind groups
- Starting a business

- Writing a blog, novel, or memoir
- Working with a coach or mentor
- Checking items off your Big Dreams list

MOTIVATIONAL EDUCATION

*"People often say that motivation doesn't last.
Well, neither does bathing—that's why we recommend it daily."*

~ Zig Ziglar ~

Jim Rohn was fond of saying, "Negative is normal." Because negative is the normal state of the world, we must work with it. I cannot motivate Life Mastery clients enough to keep them fired up from one session to the next, so I require them to read or listen to something motivational every day. The ideal system to keep your passion for progress animated is to read motivational material at home or work every day, and to listen to an inspiring audiobook as you commute. We must swim upstream to keep the negativity from derailing our dreams. A daily habit of self-motivation is fundamental to keep your enthusiasm high for accomplishment, so make sure you write that one down in your notes.

Another classic statement from Jim Rohn, and one he repeated often, is, "There are no new fundamentals. You've got to be a little suspicious of someone who says, 'I've got a new fundamental.' That's like someone inviting you to tour a factory where they are manufacturing antiques." There are many inspiring people who have left their mark on my life, and Jim Rohn is among those who have impacted me the most. I highly recommend any of his audiobooks. There are also many motivational books that are classics and the foundation of the careers of modern-day motivators, including Jim Rohn. These books have stood the test of time, and they are a good place to start. Here are a few classics you don't want to miss:

SHERRY STIRLING FERNANDEZ

- *As a Man Thinketh* by James Allen
- *Think and Grow Rich* by Napoleon Hill
- *How to Win Friends and Influence People* by Dale Carnegie
- *The Strangest Secret* by Earl Nightingale
- *See You at the Top* by Zig Ziglar
- *The Greatest Salesman in the World* by Og Mandino
- *The 7 Habits of Highly Effective People* by Stephen R. Covey
- *The Power of Positive Thinking* by Norman Vincent Peale
- *The Magic of Thinking Big* by David J. Schwartz
- *Man's Search for Meaning* by Viktor Frankl
- *The Richest Man in Babylon* by George S. Clason

The Compound Effect by Darren Hardy is typically the first book I recommend to clients because it supports the Life Mastery concepts. It isn't quite a classic yet, but I recommend you read it as well.

James Bryce said, "The worth of a book is to be measured by what you can carry away from it." Not every book you pick up will be dazzling in its ability to inspire you. That is okay. If you get one good idea out of a book and apply it, the book was well worth your time. One technique that has been extremely useful to me is that when I read a book, I underline everything that speaks to me in any way—every good idea, new thought, and inspiring sentiment. Then when I have finished the book, I write those things in a journal. By writing them, they become more solidly a part of my working knowledge. I get to review the ideas, remember things I have forgotten, and be inspired all over again. When that journal is full, I have a book to read where every word is inspiring to me. I have referred to those journals many times for inspiration and information as I have written *Life Mastery: Personal Progression Toward an Infinite Potential.*

Motivation can also be found in a simple sentence. Maybe you have wondered about my liberal use of quotations. I have collected wise, pithy little aphorisms since my teenage years. This practice began in high school with a teacher who put a quote on the board each day and required that we write them in a designated notebook. I have many of these quotes memorized, and they are like old friends to me. They keep me motivated, and they serve me in times of need. I now have hundreds of collected quotations, which I have put into a compilation and given to friends and family. That collection will soon be revised and available for purchase. This simple practice has affected my life more than anything I learned in high school, and I cannot even remember the teacher's name. If someone from Snake River High School in Idaho reads this, maybe they can remember the teacher's name and let me know. I would love to thank him.

THE NEWS

"The culture of news is a culture without nuance."

~ Maria Popova ~

There was a time when we only had the five o'clock news and the ten o'clock news. Including sports and weather, the news was thirty minutes and typically without commentary. The ten o'clock news was a repeat of the five o'clock, so you only watched one or the other. The news was almost exactly the same on all three channels, so it didn't matter which one you watched. Now, we can watch the news twenty-four hours a day, seven days a week. The news is sensationalized and commentated on at length, and the programs are at odds with one another. The modern news program is designed to whip up undue emotion and leaves viewers wringing their hands about the unfairness of the past and fearing for the future. Non-stop news programs are adding a boatload of negativity to an already negative world.

In 2018, we traveled to Jordan and Israel. Before we left for these Middle Eastern countries, we were frequently asked if we were afraid to go. While we were there, we received texts from family and friends, asking if we were okay, because there had been some reports on the news about violence in Israel. Israel was peaceful, and we always felt safe. While there, we learned that the chances of dying violently in Israel are far less than in the state of Utah. The everyday citizens, both Arabs and Jews, work and live peacefully with each other. The political climate, technology, and the economy were all a surprise. The Israel I encountered was not the one I expected. This experience clarified something we already suspected: The news media doesn't paint the complete picture.

News and news commentaries are a drain on your time and your creativity. You will be surprised how well you can get by without them. In September of 2019, my sister Jamie, our daughter Summer, grandson Brady, Ken, and I hiked the Tour du Mont Blanc. We spent twelve days in the Alps, and ten of those days we hiked from morning until evening. With travel and sightseeing, the entire trip was seventeen days. I heard little news during those seventeen days, so I was curious to get home and see what I had missed. When I arrived home, I discovered that nothing noteworthy had happened. And yet, every day I was gone, the words "BREAKING NEWS" rolled across the screens of television sets across America, just like it does every day.

The news is deliberately designed to sound critically important in the moment, but how important is it in the whole context of your life? Do not give the "talking heads" a chance to wind you up, leave you in despair, or addict you to anger. There was a time when I would have our newspapers saved when I traveled so I could read them when I arrived home. I didn't want to miss anything, especially locally. It turned out that all I missed was the time I wasted reading them. Read just enough of the headlines so you are not caught off-guard and seek the news that is relevant to your fields of endeavor. There are apps that filter news so you only receive the information you need or want.

READING FICTION

"How many a man has dated a new era in his life from the reading of a book."

~ Henry David Thoreau ~

In a book group discussion, a member said they had no time to read a recommended book of fiction because they needed to spend all their reading time on educational material in their field. I can relate to that feeling because when I owned FitMania, I felt similar pressure. I have also gained much from fiction, including insights I could not have learned as well in a manual. Fiction connects the emotional and mental self, allowing you to see the world more clearly.

My love of books was greatly advanced when I was eleven. There was an actual gang in the school where I attended sixth grade. This wasn't a school in some hard-bitten inner city, but in the small town of Idaho Falls in Idaho. These sixth-grade kids would randomly choose another student and wait for them after school so they could "beat them up." One day it was my turn. I was still new to the school, so it was inevitable. They waited for me in an alley I had to pass on my way home. When I realized what was happening, I was terrified! Fortunately, some parents chased them off, and one ran to get my mother. I do not know whose idea it was, but the next day I was asked to work in the school library for thirty minutes a day after school. It solved my problem with the gang because they were not that patient, but what really rocked my world was how my love of books exploded! I had always enjoyed reading, but now I was learning to simply love books.

Later, when I was thirteen, I read *Jane Eyre,* by Charlotte Bronte, and it was the beginning of my love for the classics. I had been collecting leather-bound classics for decades before Ken started plowing through my collection. As he read, he would find passages he thought were especially well-written and read them to me. Ken especially loved Mary Shelley's *Frankenstein* and would read the few ending paragraphs to anyone who showed an interest. He keeps a "book journal," and this is what he wrote about Shelley's *Frankenstein*:

"When I was a young teenager, I read Mary Shelley's Frankenstein. Boy did that ever add to my fears. Never was a monster more frightening to me than that horrid creation, killing everyone who got in his way. As a young person, I totally missed the point of that book. I recently read it again and I loved it. Frankenstein's monster was still the same hideous creature that lurked in the dark places in my mind, but now I understood what Mary Shelley was trying to say in her marvelous classic. This was a story about prejudice. This was a being who, like all of us, just wanted to be loved. He watched and learned from old man DeLacey and his family about love and caring. It was what he desired for himself but knew he could never have because he was different. The people judged the monster on his appearance, but all he wanted was to love and be loved. The last few pages of this book, in my opinion, are some of the most powerful and well-written literature that exists."

Now that you have given up watching the news, you have some extra time and mental energy. Try using it to read a little more fiction. Here are some benefits of reading fiction:

- Builds empathy and understanding of people you have never met and places you have never visited.
- Develops human context for understanding world history.
- Increases vocabulary and improves the use of language.
- Forms new ideas and new things to think about.
- Develops creativity.
- Is a release for stress because it disengages the mind (reading has been shown to have similar effects on our mind as meditation).
- Assists you in becoming a better conversationalist.
- Improves memory.
- To be well-read is to be well-educated.
- It's fun!

Knowledge and education have been a theme throughout this book and will continue to be so. This chapter has focused on reading, but reading is just one way to learn things. Less intentional learning comes from the experiences of life, for every life experience has the seeds of new knowledge in it. The question is not whether we will learn in this life—learning is inevitable. We can leave to chance what we will learn, how much we will learn, and how we will apply it, or we can determine what we want to be and direct our learning to that end. Jan Vanek says it better than I ever could: "You are the books you read, the films you watch, the music you listen to, the people you meet, the dreams you have, the conversations you engage in. You are what you take from these. You are the sound of the ocean, the breath of fresh air, the brightest light and the darkest corner. You are a collective of every experience you have had in your life. So drown yourself in a sea of knowledge and existence. Let the words run through your veins and let the colors fill your mind."

REFLECTIVE QUESTIONS

- What am I truly curious about?
- Do I spend too much time and emotional energy consuming contentious news commentary?
- Do I actively curate a list of books I want to read?
- Is my library a reflection of the person I want to be?

8

LIFE MASTERY IN VOCATION, MONEY, AND LIFESTYLE

S etting goals in these three areas of Life Mastery is easy. They are also closely intertwined and often cross over each other. Like the previous sections, this one is designed to give you ideas about goals to set and to get you thinking about changes that need to be made. Remember to write down the ideas that come to you.

VOCATION

Vocation can be defined in many ways. Some people may feel they have had a clarion call to a certain profession since they were young. Some may stumble into a field they love and think of it as a calling. Most people have a job that pays the bills, and with a little luck or the right attitude, is satisfying enough for now. In this chapter, vocation is defined by what you do during your "workday." For most people, it is their employment, but not everyone works for a paycheck. Many retired people spend much of their day volunteering, working on hobbies, mentoring, or dabbling in financial projects. One reason to retire is so we can be productive in the ways we would like to be, instead of the ways we have to be in order to get a paycheck. For some, their vocation may be the full-time care of their children and home. Vocation is one of the eight areas of Life Mastery, and when it's given direction and planning, it becomes an opportunity for increased happiness by *personal progression toward and infinite potential.*

A ROUTINE FOR SUCCESS

"For the happiest life, days should be rigorously planned, nights left open to chance."

~ Mignon McLaughlin ~

Just as your life must be designed for success, so must your days. The secret to having successful days is the same as the secret to having a successful life. It is good planning and a routine of success-driven habits. If you study the lives of successful people, you will find that, typically, they plan their day so that it looks something like this:

- Early morning. This time is for personal development. Set your alarm so you have plenty of time to work on personal daily habits and goals. This is the time to read, meditate, exercise, write goals, etc. Once the workday starts, it's too late to plan it, so it is also important to spend a few minutes planning the day. This morning time must have a rigid routine, and nothing else should take precedence. Holding this time for yourself inviolate is not selfish. The best thing you can do for your spouse, children, or company is to be a better you, and that requires some sacred time for growth. Besides the development of habits and opportunity for personal growth, having a tight routine in the morning will allow you to feel more control over your day.
- Day time. It is essential for human happiness to spend our days being productive. Therefore, we must work, and that work is our vocation. For most people, this means a job, business,

calling, or career. It can also mean homemaker, mother, father, or volunteer. If you are retired, it might mean hobbies and activities. This is the time of the day we contribute to society and make the world better for our efforts.

- Evening. "For the happiest life, days should be rigorously planned, nights left open to chance," according to Mignon McLaughlin. An evening routine is also important but can be less strict than the morning routine. This time is devoted to relationships. Have a family dinner or eat with friends. Eating is a social time, and the evening meal is especially so. Other good activities are helping with your children's homework, reading to your children, and some quality time with a beloved life partner. Then go to bed at a reasonable time. Occasionally, this evening routine is replaced with a date night or time with friends. If your family has so many activities that you cannot do some of these other important things routinely, then simplify. Time together is more important than spending every evening at the playing field. Some chores can be done as a family, but if your evenings are too full of household chores, downsize or hire someone to take care of a few things. Remember, this is your relationship time. The lawn has to be mowed, but you won't go to your grave with regrets about not having mowed the lawn.

PLAN YOUR WORKDAY

"I got the blues thinking of the future, so I left off and made some marmalade. It's amazing how it cheers one up to shred oranges and scrub the floor."

~ D.H. Lawrence ~

If Adam and his posterity had been able to live without working, the human race would never have survived. We need work to sustain ourselves financially, and we need work to feel productive and useful. The trick is to have work that is satisfying, supports us financially, and facilitates the fulfilling of our BIG DREAMS. But most people walk through their workday, the time when productivity should be highest, without a plan. They are like Alice when she went through the looking glass in the book by Lewis Carroll:

> Alice: "Would you tell me, please, which way I ought to go from here?"
> Cheshire Cat: "That depends a good deal on where you want to get to."
> Alice: "I don't much care where—"
> Cheshire Cat: "Then it doesn't matter which way you go."

Do not let this be you. You have big dreams, and to make those dreams come true, every single day matters. And to make every day matter, it must be planned in advance. Without planning, you can spend your day putting out fires, answering emails, and spending too much time with the energy vampires that lurk everywhere. Here are a few suggestions to organize your workday:

- Plan your day the night before or first thing in the morning. Determine what your top three priorities are for the day. They should be consistent with your top three priorities for the week, the current ninety days, the year, and so on.
- Returning messages can drain your time and give a false sense of productivity. Schedule a time to return emails, phone calls, and texts. For example, you might check messages at 9:00 am to catch the things that need to be handled for that day and then again at 4:00 pm to see what might be critical before you leave for the day. If you do this consistently, you will train people to expect responses at certain times, and they will be less likely to interrupt your day. Messages that might have seemed urgent in the moment will often be resolved by the time you get to them.

- Be flexible. Have a plan A, but because we work with other mortals, some days, you may need to regroup and make a plan B, or even a plan C.
- Plan chunks of time through the day where you can do deep work without interruption. Turn off your phone and let the people you work with know you will be unavailable. For more about deep work, I recommend Cal Newport's book, *Deep Work: Rules for Focused Success in a Distracted World.*
- Determine the items that are most important each day and then do the ones first you dread most. At FitMania, the staff and I would remind each other to "eat that frog," which we borrowed from Mark Twain's comment: "If it's your job to eat a frog, it's best to do it first thing in the morning. And if it's your job to eat two frogs, it's best to eat the biggest one first."
- I learned from Lou Holtz to regularly ask myself, "What's important now?" When you are between tasks or suspect you are off-track, stop and ask yourself, "What's important now?"
- It is easy to get caught in the trap of more time at work equals more success, but it doesn't. Work smart all day and when the workday is over, go home.
- Take regular vacations. Skipping vacations won't help your success in the long run. Vacations "sharpen the saw."

BE AN EXPERT IN YOUR FIELD

"My parents always taught me that my day job would never make me rich. It'd be my homework."

~ Daymond John ~

A few years ago, a woman hit all the social media and talk shows touting a small plastic instrument she claimed would remove cellulite and do other wondrous things. It was the latest magic pill for excess body fat. I know enough about physiology to know there was no way it was removing cellulite. Fascia fibers are extremely strong, and to "break up fascia" would require so much force that the body would sustain serious injury. Users were showing off their bruises with pride and still not using enough force to "break up fascia," which is good because fascia should not have been broken up in the first place. I did my research to confirm what I knew, and I bought one to prove it didn't work. I commented on every social media post on the topic, advising people not to buy it. I wrote to the woman who supposedly invented it and begged my clients not to fall for this gimmick. Still, I know a lot of smart people who bought it, hoping it was the solution to their problems, and suffered another disappointment. Unfortunately, this is not an isolated instance. There is a continuous onslaught of purveyors of false information, pills, diets, snake oils, and gimmicks that sickeningly prey on people desperate for a solution. When people ask me about the latest diet or fitness trend, it isn't enough that I know it is wrong; I have to be able to explain why it is wrong. That means good knowledge of physiology, staying current with the latest information, looking at the studies, and knowing what the latest trends are. If I want to be a leader in my field—if I want people to see me as credible—I need to be prepared.

Whatever your field or arena of influence, you have a similar need to be continually educating yourself. If you want expert status in your field, then you must have the most pertinent information. Read the books and periodicals in your field and attend as many lectures, seminars, and workshops as you can. Do your homework, and people will be looking to you when they need answers.

If you own a business, then you absolutely must be current in your field and in business practices. Too many people have a passion for what they do, and do it well, but fail because they don't understand how to successfully run a business. If you do not know how to run a business, then it will be difficult to make any business profitable. If you do, you can make any business thrive. Business coaches can be a godsend, and good ones are easy to find. Remember, there is a difference between theory and practice, so look for a business coach who has successfully run a few businesses.

MONEY

"It is the desire of God that you should get rich. He wants you to get rich because he can express himself better through you if you have plenty of things to use in giving him expression. He can live more in you if you have unlimited command of the means of life."

~ Wallace D. Wattle ~

It's been said, "Money can't buy happiness, but it does enable one to pick out the particular kind of misery that he enjoys the most," and that has some truth. On the other hand, it's been pointed out that, "If someone can't buy happiness with money, it must be that they don't know where to shop."

Is the accumulation of wealth a righteous pursuit? I asked this question to a group of teenagers and adults. Nearly all the teens said yes, but a disturbing number of the adults said no. I am always surprised at how some people dismiss the accumulation of wealth as evil, and even staunchly defend poverty as noble. Money is referred to as "filthy lucre," and we worry that the love of money is the root of all evil. I have been on both ends of wealth as a child, and again as an adult. I can assure you there is nothing particularly noble about being poor. It's as easy to become obsessed with money when you don't have enough of it as it is when you have a lot.

The criticism of wealth is loudest from those who do not have it, and do not expect to get it. There is a sense that there isn't enough money to go around. Jim Rohn put it this way: "Wealth is like the ocean. There is plenty for everyone, but some people come to the ocean with a teaspoon." The world is full of possibilities, and everyone can be wealthy.

We know a man who is currently in his seventies. He worked hard and faithfully at his employment all his working life. Now he lives in subsidized housing and serves at the Senior Center, where the free lunch he receives helps him make ends meet. This is a lifestyle, but not the kind we dream of. If this man had invested only fifty dollars a month during his working life, then his retirement income would have doubled and exceeded his income while working. How would that have affected his lifestyle? That is just one of many small choices he could have made toward being financially independent and a lifestyle that would have exceeded his dreams. This story is not unique.

Most people would like to be wealthy, and you probably would not be reading this book if you did not believe that. However, if you need some reasons to convince yourself that seeking wealth is a wholesome endeavor, then here are a few:

- Development of new skills in the attainment of wealth. Jim Rohn frequently said, "Become a millionaire not for the million dollars, but for what it will make of you to achieve it."
- Freedom from financial worry.
- Freedom to work doing what you love instead of what you have to.
- Freedom to travel.
- Better access to meet new people.
- Better options for education for yourself and your family.
- Freedom to serve. Wallace D. Wattle said, "Love is denied expression by poverty."
- The means to give. The philanthropy of citizens does far more good in the world than government welfare.
- It is a measure of success.
- To contribute to the national and world economy through your own enterprise. George S. Clason wrote, "Our prosperity as a nation depends upon the personal financial prosperity of each of us as individuals."
- For the joy of achievement.

The reason money gets a bad rap is that too many people have pursued wealth without ethics and for the wrong reasons. It is fine to be pleased with your accomplishments, including the accumulation of money, but money attained at the expense of your principles or your relationships will not bring satisfaction or happiness. Here are a few basic principles for wealth:

- Never sacrifice your integrity for money.
- Use sound financial principles for attaining wealth.
- Keep your life in balance, maintaining your health, relationships, and spiritual life; otherwise, your riches may cost you too much.

How much money do you need to consider yourself wealthy? Everyone will have their own definition of wealth. Who can be wealthy? Anyone can be wealthy. People who have lived on meager incomes have retired wealthy. My in-laws are a good example. They started with little, but they worked hard, managed their finances well, and were able to retire in their early fifties. They lived comfortably, and when they died, they left an inheritance for their children. A retired schoolteacher lived simply and died with a million dollars under her mattress. Conversely, we find athletes, movie stars, and lottery winners who end up broke. It isn't how much money a person makes but how they perceive money, and how they use it, that makes the difference. Ayn Rand wrote, "Money is only a tool. It will take you wherever you wish, but it will not replace you as the driver."

Like all Life Mastery principles, the possibilities for financial success are without limit. Here are six major rules for personal finances:

- Have a budget. Time and money are the same in at least one regard: Unless we track it, we don't know how much we are wasting. And there are apps for both. Ken works with people on their finances as a mentor and coach. In every case where they have no budget, Ken finds they have money they didn't know they had. Money that couldn't be accounted for. If you do not have a good budget, then you are almost certainly in the same situation. What if that money was discovered and invested?
- Save. If you are so dirt poor that you can hardly feed yourself, still save something. You will feel less impoverished, and with time it will change how you view money. It will create the habit of saving and improve your self-discipline. If you wait until you get that raise, or that bonus, or until that

bill is paid, then you will never do it. It is like that fitness goal that is going to start on Monday. There will always be another excuse.

- Give 10% of your income to charity. Do not wait until you have a lot of money to begin doing this. If you can't be generous when it is hard, you won't be generous when it is easy. Besides being the right thing to do, there is some law in the universe that is put to work when we are generous. Every successful person I have ever admired has followed this 10% rule and believed this practice contributed to their success. If you are not sure, take a leap of faith and test it for six months.

- Develop a team. Start immediately with an investment advisor. Other team members might be CPAs, real estate agents, and bankers. These people should be successful professionals who you can trust and can access easily with questions.

- Do not go into debt for anything except a house or to have a baby if your insurance won't cover it (some things can't be measured in money). You may need to borrow for an inexpensive used car, but only as a last resort.

- Have life insurance until you are financially independent. Don't think in terms of what you earn but in terms of what it would cost to replace you. When our family was young, I was a full-time homemaker to our large family. While I did not bring in an income, we had life insurance on both of us. We needed an income if something happened to Ken. If I died or was incapacitated, Ken would either have to quit working or hire someone full time to care for our children. We planned for both.

- Have an updated will and testament.

Some other good ideas:

- Experiences are more valuable than things. Take more vacations and accumulate less stuff. Stuff doesn't build memories. In the late 1990s, our finances had loosened up, and we were able to travel and had taken our kids on some pretty nice adventures, but it was still a stress on the budget. A rare book had come into our possession, and after a few years, I decided it needed to get into the hands of professionals, so I put it up for sale on a site where collectors bid for such things. It sold for an unexpected $20,000! We used the money to take our kids on a fifteen-day car trip to Belize. Belize wasn't as touristy as it is now, and it was the off-season, so we were able to make up the trip as we went along. It was the adventure of a lifetime!

- In a marriage, budgeting is a joint project, but whoever is best with money is the best person to handle the day-to-day finances.
- It becomes less practical all the time, but always use cash if you can. You will spend less because you feel the loss more fully, and it creates an automatic budget because when it's gone, it's gone. A study conducted by Dun & Bradstreet found that people spend 12–18% more when using credit cards instead of cash. McDonald's reports its average ticket is $7 when people use credit cards versus $4.50 for cash. A debit card might be better, but I suspect some of the same psychology exists using either kind of plastic.

LIFESTYLE

"If you don't design your own life plan, chances are you'll fall into someone else's plan. And guess what they have planned for you? Not much."

~ Jim Rohn ~

In the Gospel of Luke, a story is told of a rich man who had such a plentiful harvest that he hardly had room to store his abundance. He decides to tear down the old barns and build bigger ones. His plan is to fill the bigger barns with his riches, and once that is done, he will take his ease and be merry. The rich man never realizes his dream because he dies that very night. God calls him a fool, not because he had spent his life acquiring wealth, but because he had postponed rejoicing in the fruits of his labor until it was too late. He hadn't taken the time to enjoy his success before seeking more. Remember the formula *contentment + progress = happiness?* Life is not only meant to be improved, but also to be savored. A few of the benefits of relishing the journey include the following:

- Maintaining balance in the quest for achievement.
- Provides a feeling of contentment with life.
- Life is a gift and enjoying a gift is an expression of gratitude.
- Another path to realizing our infinite potential. The more fully we live, the more we become.
- No regrets. We don't want to be like the man with the barns.

In Life Mastery, we refer to the savoring of the journey as Lifestyle. Lifestyle, as an area of Life Mastery, is not your plans for retirement—neither is it about creating excess idle time. There is no growth, and so no happiness, in idleness. Lifestyle is enjoying the journey. It is taking pleasure in what we have, celebrating our successes, and living consciously and joyfully. Like all areas of Life Mastery, having command of your lifestyle will require planning. "Stop and smell the roses" is a cliché, but it is also a good motto for planning Lifestyle goals. A joyful and rewarding lifestyle includes planning for the following:

- Service.
- Enjoying relationships.
- Connecting with nature.
- Enjoying hobbies.
- Travel.
- Time alone to think or wander.

A healthy lifestyle does not stand alone but is enhanced by the balanced progress in each of the areas of Life Mastery. Having self-respect, the respect of others, good health, spiritual fulfillment, and an educated mind are all important to a fulfilling lifestyle.

The lifestyle Ken and I *designed* is simple and easy living. We live in a downtown condo. There is no yard to mow, windows to wash, or roofs to fix. We walk to our bank, accountant, lawyer, and to dinner. We live near the river, and close to hiking trails. This simple living provides us with the time to serve, spend with our family, and travel. It also makes it possible for us to give more time to personal growth and to speak, coach, and mentor. In order to work and earn money for school, our grandson, Isaac, spent the summer he turned nineteen living with us. When he wasn't working, the three of us spent a lot of time together. As he observed our way of life, I could see him taking mental notes on what he wants his own lifestyle to look like.

There are no ordinary moments, and every minute of every single day matters. Do not wait to take your ease and be merry.

QUESTIONS FOR REFLECTION

- Are my days well planned?
- Am I financially disciplined and confident?
- How much money would I need to consider myself financially independent?
- Is my lifestyle designed or accidental?

9

LIFE MASTERY AND CHARACTER

WE LOVE PEOPLE OF STRENGTH

"Parents can only give good advice, but the final forming of a person's character lies in their own hands."

~ Ann Frank ~

People are drawn to the strength of other people. I realized the extent of this phenomenon in a single moment. It was a small thing, but the memory can still make me a little emotional. We held two or three fitness challenges a year while I owned FitMania. We were at the end of one of those first challenges and were scurrying around doing our various jobs, which included getting clients ready for "after" pictures with a professional photographer. Kacey was a client in the early days and quickly moved to training classes and helping me grow FitMania. Kacey was also participating in this particular challenge. She was a strong and athletic woman, and during the ninety-day challenge, she had become lean and even stronger. She was wearing a modest version of the suggested two-piece swimsuit and was doing a few exercises to pump up. I can still see her doing pushups in the middle of the busyness when a hush slowly crept across the room. One by one, we had each stopped to watch. We had become mesmerized by the beauty of her strength. This wasn't Baywatch beauty—all siliconed, sexed-up, and air-brushed—this was strength that was authentically beautiful, and we were all attracted to it. Even as I write this, I am overcome with some of the same emotion I felt that day. Had she been muscular because of steroids or lean by artificial means, we would not have experienced such awe. Kacey's strength was authentic and inspiring.

We are similarly attracted to authentic spiritual strength. We may think the lady who macramé's with her toes and worships her cat is entertaining, or a charismatic leader might hold our attention for a moment, but when we begin a sincere search for spirituality, we recognize authentic spiritual strength and are repelled by imposters. Wisdom is a strength. One is wise because of a relentless search for truth discovered, applied, and refined. If we are also searchers for truth, we will find the wise soul compelling but the imitator distracting.

If there is one strength more compelling than the others, it is the strength of character. People who are strong enough to stand up for what is right. We are attracted to people with authentic strength of character but have disdain for hypocrites. This is why we love heroes and superheroes. And it is this strength of character upon which all other strengths must be built.

Character and integrity are used interchangeably, which works most of the time, but they are different. Character is our moral and ethical code, and integrity means we live according to that code. Thus, someone who lives with integrity consistently becomes a person of character and lives according to their moral values. However, there is a gap between what we believe and what we do. It is the *integrity gap,* and it always exists. It is the mortal condition. The person of character is always working to narrow the *integrity gap.* The smaller the gap between our deepest convictions and our actions, the greater our integrity and our character. The purpose of this book is to inspire readers toward a happy and fulfilled life. There simply can be no happiness if what we do is not aligned with our deepest convictions. A person of high character acts with integrity in public, but the highest test of character is what we do when no one is watching.

We often talk about people who have great moral character as if they were born that way. Character, integrity, honor—these are not gifts. These are victories. And how are they won? Lincoln said, "I do the very best I know how—the very best I can; and I mean to keep doing so until the end." That is how. We just keep doing our very best to live what we believe and never quit. We must always be looking for the cracks in our character and striving to be better.

But it isn't solely the grind to be better that builds character. To surround ourselves with people of integrity, to love well, to be inspired by books, sermons, poetry, music, and great art strengthens our moral fiber. In *The Road to Character*, David Brooks makes this observation:

> "Character is not only built through austerity and hardship. It is also built sweetly through love and pleasure. When you have deep friendships with good people, you copy and absorb some of their best traits. When you love a person deeply, you want to serve them and earn their regard. When you experience great art, you widen your repertoire of emotions. Through your devotion to some cause, you elevate your desires and organize your energies."[6]

We are inspired by great acts of heroism. The integrity to stand up against all odds is the stuff of history, books, and movies. But character is not built in these moments—it is revealed. The traits of heroism, character, and integrity are developed slowly by our day-to-day actions. It is the bundling together of thousands of tiny choices that make us who we are.

---

[6] David Brooks, *The Road to Character* (New York: Random House, 2015), 12.

SHERRY STIRLING FERNANDEZ

STRIVE FOR EXCELLENCE

*"If a man is called to be a street sweeper, he should sweep
streets even as Michelangelo painted, or Beethoven composed music,
or Shakespeare wrote poetry. He should sweep streets so well
that all the hosts of heaven and Earth will pause to say, here lived a
great street sweeper who did his job well."*

~ Martin Luther King, Jr. ~

Excellence is the opposite of perfection. Perfection is external. It competes with others to be the best. Excellence is internal. It competes with self. It is trying to be a little better today than yesterday. It is doing our best and being our best in the details of life. For example, in his later years, a well-respected and successful man was dying of cancer and bedridden. Still, with help and great effort, he got dressed every morning. With help and great effort, he made his bed and then laid on top of it. That is excellence. Excellence is putting our shopping cart away, and maybe someone else's as well. It is picking up a piece of litter, it is dressing our best regardless of who we might see, it is speaking well of others, and a thousand other things.

Excellence is the essence of character. There is a cost involved when you put away your shopping cart or turn off Netflix. And we must be willing to pay the price to become something better. Great athletes and great coaches understand this. Former Notre Dame football coach, Lou Holtz, taught, "Do everything to the best of your abilities. When you lower standards, you only invite mediocrity." And Vince Lombardi said, "The quality of a person's life is in direct proportion to their commitment to excellence, regardless of their chosen field of endeavor." See yourself as a world-class athlete on the playing field of life striving for excellence. You only have this one life to get it right, and life is too short to be anything but your best every day. Some days will be harder than others, and you will meet circumstances that might try your commitment. On those occasions, challenge yourself to do your best to live with excellence for the next five minutes. And then the next. It gets the ball rolling.

162

DEVELOP SELF-DISCIPLINE

*"Most people don't want to engage in these extra disciplines
but the treasure and the equity is so unique! The price paid in these early
disciplines is small compared to the treasures that will unfold for you
in your heart, your mind and your purse."*

~ Jim Rohn ~

From the wisdom of Proverbs, we are told, "He that hath no rule over his own spirit is like a city that is broken down, and without walls." Self-discipline is both a hallmark of character and the means by which we develop character as well as every other discipline, good habit, and virtue. It is also how we meet every goal. Without discipline, there is no progress and therefore only limited happiness, if there is happiness at all.

About twenty-five years ago, a man who has been a good friend for decades asked me to come to his office. I was a little surprised at the formality of his request, but also a little intrigued. Once in his office, the first thing he did was to ask me, "How do you develop self-discipline?" I was caught off-guard and fumbled for an answer. I have thought about that question frequently over the years. I have a ready answer now: *Self-discipline is like a muscle. The more you use it, the more it grows. And one discipline builds on another.* If the only daily discipline I have is brushing my teeth, then I will add one desired discipline to that habit faithfully until the new one becomes a habit. I connect them in my mind so that when I think of brushing my teeth, I think of my new desired habit. When I have that one down, I add another desired discipline until it is a habit.

I brush my teeth.
I brush my teeth and eat a healthy breakfast.
I brush my teeth, eat a healthy breakfast, and read something motivational.
I brush my teeth, eat breakfast, read something motivational, and exercise.

I am becoming more disciplined every day, and I am becoming a better person because my teeth are clean, my diet is better, my mind full of positive things to keep me going, and my body is stronger. Does this take time? Yes! And a lot of it. Does it take effort? A boat-load of effort! Is it worth it? Oh yes!

Developing good habits is critical to all success, including the development of character. Every principle will require some self-discipline to become better.

BE HONEST IN SPEECH

"We tell lies when we are afraid... afraid of what we don't know, afraid of what others will think, afraid of what will be found out about us. But every time we tell a lie, the thing that we fear grows stronger."

~ Tad Williams ~

In my senior year of high school, I bullied an insecure teacher into giving me a part in the school play. Besides being a rude thing to do, I was a horrible actor. It was not my finest moment. I was very good at debate, and somehow I thought if I could debate, I could act, but I was embarrassingly mistaken. I cannot act and hold a straight face. To lie, you must put on an act, so not only can I not act, but I also cannot tell a straight-up lie with any success. But there is more to being honest in speech than simply not telling bald-faced lies. I come from a family where exaggeration and hyperbole is normal conversation, and I am prone to that kind of lying. It was an audio-book by Wayne Dyer that made me realize it was a problem when he said something like, *strive to make everything you say be exactly as it is.* I knew my speech was full of untruths, and I resolved in that moment to make changes. Think about the kinds of phrases that are common in our everyday speech. Do you use phrases like these?

Everyone thinks that _____. (Everyone?)

I have said a thousand times that _____. (A thousand?)
People are _____. (All people?)
Every time I _____. (Every time?)

Other ways our speech can be dishonest is to say nothing and allow a misconception, or to make an excuse that puts the blame on someone or something else.

BE HONEST IN FINANCES

"There is no such thing as a minor lapse of integrity."

~ Tom Peters ~

We started our construction supply business in the 1980s. Our business was still new and struggling when Ken placed an order for twelve of a certain item and received twelve cases of that item by accident. When he told me, in another less than shining moment, I said, "Think of the great profit margin we will have on those!" He looked at me like I was an alien! We have always been scrupulously honest in our financial dealings, and we both believe honesty is an important factor in a successful life. Pay your bills. Pay your taxes. Be above suspicion in all your financial dealings. The easiest place to compromise our integrity is when it comes to the dealing of money.

KEEP PROMISES

"The woods are lovely, dark and deep.
But I have promises to keep,
And miles to go before I sleep,
And miles to go before I sleep."

~ Robert Frost ~

I read a lot of books on parenting in a determined effort to raise my children differently than the way my siblings and I were raised. One book, the title long forgotten, said something about keeping promises to your children. I do not remember the exact words used, but it must have been good. It left me forever committed to keeping my promises to my children. The seriousness of keeping promises has carried over into all my relationships. For that reason, I am slow to make a promise. People in my world will occasionally be frustrated when they cannot get an immediate commitment from me, but I need to be fully committed to anything I agree to, because once I say I will do a thing, I will do my very best to do it. Avoid breaking promises or canceling events if it can be helped. Integrity is important, and you cannot be both credible and flakey at the same time. Norman Vincent Peale said it cleverly: "Promises are like crying babies in a theater; they should be carried out at once."

BE ON TIME

"Better three hours too soon than a minute too late."

~ William Shakespeare ~

Making an appointment with anyone for any reason is a promise. I was in a three-day experiential training for personal development, and the facilitator was tough. The concept of experiential training is that you will behave in the training exercises the same way you would in real life. His philosophy was that this was our life, and he expected us to take it seriously. And we knew from the very beginning that being late was unacceptable. Period. The last day was a Saturday, and we started at 10:00 a.m. One younger man showed up solidly late. When he walked in, everyone was a little tense. No one envied him the discussion he was about to have in front of the whole group. I am sure most of the participants felt like I did, that he must have had something really serious happen. An accident, perhaps. But when asked why he was late, he said he was watching cartoons. You might laugh. We did. But I wonder if *our* excuses for being late are much better than watching cartoons.

Let's say you have agreed to meet a friend for lunch at noon at the local shopping mall. You arrive fifteen minutes late. You tell your friend how the traffic was rough, the lights were against you, you had a last-minute call, or whatever your excuse is. What will your friend say? They are kind and polite, so they will probably say something like *that is okay*, or *no problem*. They *say* that, but what do they *feel*? They almost certainly feel they are not a priority to you. You did not care about them enough to be considerate of their time. You certainly do not appear to be looking forward to spending time with them. You were essentially *watching cartoons,* and you have damaged the relationship, regardless of how polite and kind your friend is about it. Now let's say the local radio station has called, and you have won $1,000 dollars. All you have to do is to show up at noon at that same shopping mall. Will you risk being late? I doubt it. Being on time shows what we value. It is an act of integrity. Even if your friend or client is typically late, you can still show up on time. It is not about who they are but who *you* are. You are a person of character, and a person of character shows up on time.

A bonus advantage of being on time is that you will like yourself better. I have worked with clients as they break the habit of being late, and in every case, they have reported an increased sense of self-esteem.

STAND UP

"Never, 'for the sake of peace and quiet,' deny your own experience and convictions."

~ Dag Hammarskjöld ~

It can be pretty tricky to know when to stand up and when to shut up. To incite unnecessary contention is not useful. Often, we should ignore the bickering and rise above it. Anger and arguing will never help. Hate begets hate, anger begets more anger, and contention more contention. Rise above that. But sometimes we need to be a leader and be the voice that others who are more timid need. The loud voices are rarely the right ones. I often think in these cases that somebody should rise up. And then I remember I am somebody. That is the time to reflect seriously. Do I have enough information and solid judgment on the matter to be the one to speak up? When we do speak up, we must expect resistance, especially in the age of social media. *The only way to avoid criticism is to say nothing, do nothing, and be nothing.* To say, do, and be nothing is far worse than to be criticized.

Throwing a dollar in a panhandler's cup is easy. It makes the donor feel pleased with themselves, and the beggar pleased to have a dollar, but it doesn't solve anything. And it's too easy. Finding an organization that feeds the hungry, donating money until it pinches, and donating time is real help. That takes effort, and it doesn't get any press. There is none of the emotion of a crowd cheering, and you won't be on TV for your efforts, but it will make a real difference. I didn't come to understand this easily. I remember the protests of the 1960s, and I was an anti-establishment hippy in the 1970s. When we were young, my generation thought the louder the voice, the more we made a difference. With time and a search for truth, I don't see it that way anymore. Real change comes through many people doing small things. Find causes that match your passions and do something really useful. Live in a way so you will be missed when you are gone because you stood for something when you lived.

BE POLITE

"If we lose love and self respect for each other, this is how we finally die."

~ Maya Angelou ~

Being polite is a matter of kindness, consideration, and character. Good manners show respect for others and demonstrate we have self-control.

Simple things our mothers told us to say, like please and thank you, matter. Especially thank you. People will often jump through all kinds of hoops for a simple thank you. Our daughter, Katie, worked her way through school by waiting tables at an Italian restaurant. It was important to her to give her best to each customer, and she was very proud of the service she gave. On occasion, she would not be tipped, and it hurt her feelings. She would say it wasn't the money but the lack of gratitude that frustrated her. She felt that if they couldn't afford a tip, they could have at least thanked her (as her mother, my thought was that if you can't afford to tip my beautiful daughter, then stay home!). Being rude is easier than being courteous. The person who desires self-mastery will make the extra effort it takes to be courteous.

Our natural inclination is toward things that are easy, and it is easier to use crude or unrefined language than to express yourself in more dignified ways. Crude language has become mainstream, but a person of excellence can always find a better way to make a point. Profanity is unprofessional. If I know a speaker uses profanity in their presentations, then I avoid their events. It isn't because my dainty sensibilities are offended but because I expect someone who desires to motivate others to greatness to have mastered their own tongue. Profane language reveals a lack of creativity, is often angry, and always negative. Using crude language is also inconsiderate of the people around you. Language should not just lack profanity but strive to be well spoken while using good, but appropriate, vocabulary. The author and coach Robin Sharma says that to be world-class, you should have world-class language. If you want to live at the highest level, then your language must be at the highest level.

Treating a person with elevated social standing better than the proverbial janitor is common but demonstrates a lack of character. Occasionally, an employee in a retail establishment will overlook a child waiting for service in order to serve adult customers, or treat teenage customers like they are thieves. However, a person of character treats everyone with courtesy regardless of their age, race, gender, or social standing. Being polite means speaking to people, being friendly, introducing yourself, asking about others, and being gracious in an authentic way.

BE A FINISHER

"Persistence is firmly sticking to something for a prolonged period of time, even as you encounter things that try to unstick you."

~ Peter Hollins ~

There are times we commit to something we should not finish. I once signed up to take a class, but the teacher was so insulting to the students and their viewpoints that I stood up and left. About fifteen years later, I signed up for another class, and for similar reasons, I stood up and left. It wasn't until I was on my way home that I realized it was the same class with the same teacher!

Those rare exceptions aside, a person of character finishes what they start. For fourteen years, I taught an evening class for college students. The courses were on various religious topics or relationships. In most cases, no university credit was available. They came because they wanted the education. Because the classes were popular, I was scrambling to find enough chairs to seat everyone at the beginning of the semester. By the end of the semester, other responsibilities or interests would call, and almost half would drop out. After some years of this, I began giving them a little spiel at the beginning of the semester. I explained that quitting can become a habit that damages self-esteem and how there is great value in finishing something you start. I suggested they show up even if the weather was bad or if they were tired, or even if I was horribly boring (which I wasn't). That discussion helped some finish. For those who didn't finish, perhaps someday they will contrast how they feel when they finish something to how they feel when they don't. A person of character finishes what they start.

WANDERLUST

There is a small hotel in the mountain town of McCall, Idaho, called the Scandia Inn. It is one of the many projects of my niece Jade and her husband, Kyle. They put a lot of heart into the remodel with a beautiful focus on the Scandia theme. When the hotel opened, we reserved a room. As we explored the room, I discovered this poster in the bathroom:

Wan •
der
• lust

[won-der-luhst] **noun**

A strong desire or impulse to travel, wander and explore the world.

Wanderlust
A deep and uncontrollable desire to explore, a longing to travel to new and distant places around the world while gaining new experiences and appreciating new cultures

I fell in love with the word *wanderlust*. Not as a word that fits the love to travel, although that is good too, but to have *wanderlust* about all of life—to have a deep and uncontrollable desire to explore each of the significant aspects of life—the physical, the spiritual, relationships, learning, money, business, lifestyle, and the road to character with a deep and uncontrollable desire to explore, a longing to travel to new and distant places while gaining new experiences and appreciating new cultures.

QUESTIONS FOR REFLECTION

- Am I scrupulously honest?
- Do I keep my promises and finish what I start?
- What would excellence look like in my life?
- Would the people who know me best consider me to be a person of character?

PART III

HOW

To stay focused and committed to personal growth requires the strong motivation that comes from a commanding *why*. The focus of Part I: Why is a universal desire to be happy and the happiness that comes from *personal progression toward an infinite potential.* The desire to be happier, a list of Big Dreams to be fulfilled, a Personal Mission to make the world a better place, and a constitution of Governing Values to live up to, each amplify our *why*.

Personal growth can be divided into eight areas. The eight areas of Life Mastery include physical, spiritual, relationships, education, money, vocation, lifestyle, and character. Part II: What contains the information to assist you in determining *what* goals you want to set in each area.

It is frustrating to be motivated to change but not know *how* to make the needed changes. The experiential program I was involved in was excellent at assisting people in seeing where they needed to change and giving them the motivation to make changes. I became disenchanted with the program after a few years because I saw too many people who experienced life-changing breakthroughs eventually revert to old, self-defeating behaviors. They were motivated to change but not trained in *how* to achieve the desired goals and develop new habits. There are books, programs, and speakers that are excellent at motivation. What is unique about the Life Mastery program is how it provides the tools needed to turn motivation into results in every area of life. Part III: How is comprised of those tools.

Back in the time when men could make a living trapping animals, there was a man who, through mentors, trial and error, and refining what he learned along the way, learned the trade of fox trapping. He made a good living, and after a time, he became a renowned success as a trapper. After a lifetime of trapping, he began to have a desire to travel and see the world. The fox trapper amassed a sizable savings and decided to retire. One day a young man came to visit him. His desire was to have the older man teach him how to be successful in the fox trapping trade. A deal was struck, and the fox trapper sold the younger man his traps, showed him where and how to set them, and taught the young man all he knew about trapping. He then left for his journey to see the world. After a time, he returned to see how the young man was doing and discovered the young fox trapper was frustrated by his lack of success, financially destitute, and ready to quit. The old trapper asked the younger man if he had applied the methods he had been taught. The young man replied, "No, I found a better way!"

Through study, learning, practicing, and refining what I learned, I compiled the tools and systems you'll find here in Part III: How. These principles, tools, and systems are the best I have found for the successful achievement of goals and the attainment of desirable habits. I have taught them to hundreds of people who have found success directly proportionate to their effort. *Consistently applied*, the methods in this section work. Those methods include the following:

- Assessing where you are.
- Setting effective goals based on that assessment.
- Planning action steps toward the achievement of the goals you choose.
- Implementing systems to effectively execute the action steps.

10

ASSESSING WHERE YOU ARE

"When I hear somebody say, 'Life is hard,'
I am always tempted to ask, 'Compared to what?'"

~ Sydney J. Harris ~

There are a number of reasons I am grateful for cell phones, but one of the biggest is that I get lost easily, which is a gentle assessment of my problem. I have lived in the same city for over forty years, and I still find myself lost and reaching for my cell phone for help. The problem isn't that I don't know where I want to go. The problem is that I don't know where I am. Once I figure out where I am, I can find my way.

It is very difficult to successfully arrive at a destination if you are not clear about where you are when you start. The first step in establishing a program of personal progress is to take an assessment of your life. An honest assessment of your current condition will give you a clearer picture of where you are and the reality of what you are doing, as opposed to what you *think* you are doing. Richard P. Feynman said, "The first principle is that you must not fool yourself, and you are the easiest person to fool." For example, a client will tell me how important their family is and because they truly love their family, they might tell me it is a strong area of Life Mastery for them. When we look at how much time they spend working on those relationships, in comparison to work or hobbies, they realize they are not making family the priority they think they are. You cannot successfully move forward until you see clearly where you are.

There is no status quo in the universe. Every moment of your existence, you are growing into more or withering into less. As you assess your life, remember there is no status quo. Everything is growing or dying. You are getting better, or you are losing ground. Your relationships are growing, or they are dying. Your body is getting stronger or weaker. You are getting richer or poorer. You are becoming more educated or less. No status quo!

Here is an assessment tool to get you started. Take time to reflect on each question seriously. Remember, it is easy to fool yourself, so be as objective as you can. There is no need to share your assessment with anyone, but you might ask a few people who are close to you how they think you are doing in certain areas, and how you might improve. Unfortunately, some people will tell you what you want to hear, while others, when it comes to brutal honesty, take more joy in the brutality than they do in the honesty, so be sure to ask people who will be honest with you but have your best interest at heart.

After you answer the questions, then plot them on the wheel graph at the end of the assessment. There are people who tend to be pretty lenient with themselves when they answer the questions and others who are hard on themselves. Neither approach is wrong. Be more concerned about how round your wheel is rather than how big. The "flat tire" areas will indicate where more work needs to be done. Life is always in flux, and perfect balance is impossible, but avoid the condition Jim Rohn was referring to when he said, "Life without balance can cost you your relationships. Life without balance can cost you your health. Life without balance can cost you your spirituality. Life without balance can cost you your wealth and your happiness. So find things to motivate you from all areas of life. Your success depends on it."

LIFE MASTERY PERSONAL ASSESSMENT

Rate yourself in the following categories on a scale of 0 - 10: 10 being the most true and 0 being the least true — or not at all. This assessment is for your own enlightenment. Be completely honest with yourself even if the truthful response is embarrassing, painful, or in conflict with the way you see yourself.

PHYSICAL

I take responsibility for my own health.	0 1 2 3 4 5 6 7 8 9 10
I avoid processed foods including flour and sugar.	0 1 2 3 4 5 6 7 8 9 10
I eat at least four meals per day and include all three macronutrients.	0 1 2 3 4 5 6 7 8 9 10
I take the time to prepare and savor healthy foods I enjoy.	0 1 2 3 4 5 6 7 8 9 10
I drink no more than two alcoholic drinks per week.	0 1 2 3 4 5 6 7 8 9 10
I do at least 20 minutes of intense cardio at least 3x per week.	0 1 2 3 4 5 6 7 8 9 10
I do strength training at least 3x per week.	0 1 2 3 4 5 6 7 8 9 10
I take at least 10,000 steps per day.	0 1 2 3 4 5 6 7 8 9 10
I drink at least half my weight in ounces of water daily.	0 1 2 3 4 5 6 7 8 9 10
I average at least 7 hours of sleep per night.	0 1 2 3 4 5 6 7 8 9 10
Total Physical Points:	

SPIRITUAL

I take time to consider the mystical/spiritual.	0 1 2 3 4 5 6 7 8 9 10
I feel awe for the world around me.	0 1 2 3 4 5 6 7 8 9 10
I express gratitude as a way of life.	0 1 2 3 4 5 6 7 8 9 10
I study my spiritual beliefs daily.	0 1 2 3 4 5 6 7 8 9 10
I live in accordance with my spiritual beliefs.	0 1 2 3 4 5 6 7 8 9 10
I take an interest in the spiritual beliefs of others.	0 1 2 3 4 5 6 7 8 9 10
I spend time in nature at least once per week.	0 1 2 3 4 5 6 7 8 9 10
I meditate daily.	0 1 2 3 4 5 6 7 8 9 10
I serve others regularly and without thought of compensation.	0 1 2 3 4 5 6 7 8 9 10
I consider myself a spiritual person.	0 1 2 3 4 5 6 7 8 9 10
Total Spiritual Points:	

RELATIONSHIPS

I recognize my need for other people in my life.	0 1 2 3 4 5 6 7 8 9 10
I set healthy boundaries with toxic/negative people.	0 1 2 3 4 5 6 7 8 9 10
I spend time at least 10 waking hours a week with my spouse/partner.	0 1 2 3 4 5 6 7 8 9 10
I eat dinner with my family at least 4x per week.	0 1 2 3 4 5 6 7 8 9 10
I make a conscious effort to recognize the love language(s) of others.	0 1 2 3 4 5 6 7 8 9 10

I seek out association with people who are on higher ground than I am.	0 1 2 3 4 5 6 7 8 9 10
When given the choice between being right and being kind, I choose kind.	0 1 2 3 4 5 6 7 8 9 10
I listen sincerely and with interest.	0 1 2 3 4 5 6 7 8 9 10
I recognize the power of words and choose what I say carefully.	0 1 2 3 4 5 6 7 8 9 10
I do not use criticism, contempt, defensiveness, or stonewalling.	0 1 2 3 4 5 6 7 8 9 10
Total Relationships Points:	

EDUCATION AND MOTIVATION

I have a program for self-education.	0 1 2 3 4 5 6 7 8 9 10
I seek education from diverse sources.	0 1 2 3 4 5 6 7 8 9 10
I read/listen to motivational material daily.	0 1 2 3 4 5 6 7 8 9 10
I regularly use coaches or mentors.	0 1 2 3 4 5 6 7 8 9 10
I have written goals.	0 1 2 3 4 5 6 7 8 9 10
I track my progress in developing daily habits.	0 1 2 3 4 5 6 7 8 9 10
I write daily affirmations.	0 1 2 3 4 5 6 7 8 9 10
I have a written personal Mission Statement.	0 1 2 3 4 5 6 7 8 9 10
I recognize the negative influence of the news and limit the amount of news I consume.	0 1 2 3 4 5 6 7 8 9 10
I make time to read fiction as a part of my education.	0 1 2 3 4 5 6 7 8 9 10
Total Education and Motivation Points:	

VOCATION

I plan my day in advance.	0 1 2 3 4 5 6 7 8 9 10
I determine in advance what items are most important.	0 1 2 3 4 5 6 7 8 9 10
I answer emails and messages at a scheduled time.	0 1 2 3 4 5 6 7 8 9 10
I stay current with my industry news.	0 1 2 3 4 5 6 7 8 9 10
I seek to educate myself in my field daily.	0 1 2 3 4 5 6 7 8 9 10
I am continually honing my professional abilities.	0 1 2 3 4 5 6 7 8 9 10
I feel I am adequately compensated, according to my worth.	0 1 2 3 4 5 6 7 8 9 10
I leave work on time every day in order to be home with my family.	0 1 2 3 4 5 6 7 8 9 10
I take regular vacations.	0 1 2 3 4 5 6 7 8 9 10
I feel satisfaction from my vocation.	0 1 2 3 4 5 6 7 8 9 10
Total Vocation Points:	

MONEY

I have a detailed written budget and adhere to it.	0 1 2 3 4 5 6 7 8 9 10
I save 10% of my net income.	0 1 2 3 4 5 6 7 8 9 10
I give 10% of my net income to charity.	0 1 2 3 4 5 6 7 8 9 10
I have a team of professionals that assist me in attaining my financial goals.	0 1 2 3 4 5 6 7 8 9 10
I am debt free, other than my home.	0 1 2 3 4 5 6 7 8 9 10

I have adequate life insurance and medical insurance for me and my family.	0 1 2 3 4 5 6 7 8 9 10
I have an updated will and testament.	0 1 2 3 4 5 6 7 8 9 10
I have a detailed retirement fund.	0 1 2 3 4 5 6 7 8 9 10
I have a dedicated 3-month emergency fund.	0 1 2 3 4 5 6 7 8 9 10
I live within my means.	0 1 2 3 4 5 6 7 8 9 10
Total Money Points:	

LIFESTYLE

I have the time and money to support charitable causes.	0 1 2 3 4 5 6 7 8 9 10
I enjoy my relationships.	0 1 2 3 4 5 6 7 8 9 10
I have hobbies and habits that connect me with nature.	0 1 2 3 4 5 6 7 8 9 10
I have hobbies that offer me the opportunity for creativity.	0 1 2 3 4 5 6 7 8 9 10
I travel for leisure.	0 1 2 3 4 5 6 7 8 9 10
I attend cultural events regularly.	0 1 2 3 4 5 6 7 8 9 10
I take time to live in the present while planning for the future.	0 1 2 3 4 5 6 7 8 9 10
I am adding, and checking off, items on my Big Dreams list.	0 1 2 3 4 5 6 7 8 9 10
I feel there is enough time in the day to do what I both need to do, and want to do.	0 1 2 3 4 5 6 7 8 9 10
I am actively designing my lifestyle.	0 1 2 3 4 5 6 7 8 9 10
Total Lifestyle Points:	

CHARACTER

I strive for inner excellence rather than external perfection.	0 1 2 3 4 5 6 7 8 9 10
I am continually developing self-discipline.	0 1 2 3 4 5 6 7 8 9 10
I am honest in the things I say.	0 1 2 3 4 5 6 7 8 9 10
I am honest in financial matters.	0 1 2 3 4 5 6 7 8 9 10
I keep my promises.	0 1 2 3 4 5 6 7 8 9 10
I am on time professionally and personally.	0 1 2 3 4 5 6 7 8 9 10
I stand up for what I believe is right.	0 1 2 3 4 5 6 7 8 9 10
I use good manners, clean language and am courteous.	0 1 2 3 4 5 6 7 8 9 10
I finish what I start.	0 1 2 3 4 5 6 7 8 9 10
The people in my personal and professional life consider me a person of character.	0 1 2 3 4 5 6 7 8 9 10
Total Character Points:	

To see a visual assessment of where you are in your life, take your scores from the previous pages and plot them on the wheel below. Start from the center and mark one rung for every 10 points you scored in each Life Mastery area (score of 0 - 10 = 1 rung, score of 11 - 20 = 2 rungs, score of 21 – 30 = 3 rungs, etc.).

When you are finished connecting the dots and you will see how balanced your wheel is. It is hard to roll toward your infinite potential with a flat tire. Always set goals in every area but concentrate extra effort in areas where you have weaker scores.

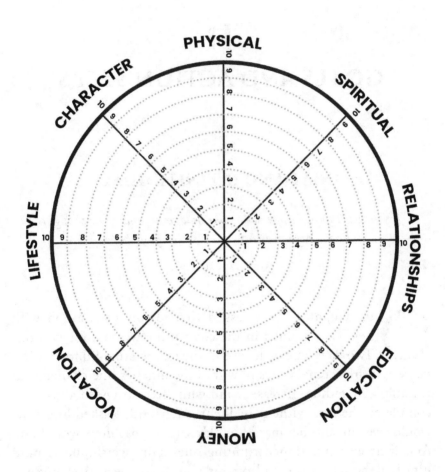

11

GOALS AND ACTION STEPS

FINITE AND INFINITE GOALS

"If you want to be happy, set a goal that commands your thoughts, liberates your energy and inspires your hopes."

~ Andrew Carnegie ~

Our daughter, Katie, asked Ken to run a marathon with her. They trained in the cool spring weather for months. Two days before the event, the temperature jumped thirty degrees. With temperatures now into the nineties, the challenge of running a marathon increased, and while Ken struggled a little, he completed the race without incident. Afterward, I asked him if he would ever run another marathon. He said he absolutely would not! And if he ever mentioned running one again, we should remind him how he felt at the end of this one. It has been twelve years, and he has never considered it, but he is proud he ran the one he did. Like Ken's marathon, some goals are of the *one-and-done* variety, or *finite* goals. Run a marathon, learn to swim, read *War and Peace*, get married, buy a house— each of these is likely to be done once and checked off. Your Big Dreams list is a list of *finite* goals. Occasionally, you will have a finite goal whose time has come, and it will find its way into your written goals with a plan and a deadline for completion. Many of your Big Dreams will be achieved in this manner. Others will be met simply because you committed your Big Dreams to writing and will more readily recognize opportunities to accomplish them.

The accomplishment of *finite* goals has varying degrees of influence on who we are becoming, depending on their level of difficulty and what we learn in accomplishing them. *Infinite* goals have a greater capacity for impact. These goals frequently require the development of habits over a long period of time, often a lifetime. The exact nature of these habits is changed, refined, and improved upon, but the habit, once established, remains. For example, training daily over your lifetime will impact your physical health and abilities, and although the type of training you do may vary, you keep training as a habit. Likewise, the amount of time you spend reading may vary, but you continue to read as a daily habit. Your meditation technique may change, but you meditate as a habit. Like Jim Rohn said, "Motivation is what gets you started. Habit is what keeps you going."

BE AUDACIOUS

You may have heard that good goals are SMART (specific, measurable, attainable, relevant, and time-bound) goals. Remember BHAGs (Big Hairy Audacious Goals)? The problem with SMART goals is that they can reduce your goals to something more mundane than audacious. There was an article in *Forbes* magazine that caught my eye. The title was *People Who Set SMART Goals Are Less Likely to Love Their Job*. In the study that was the basis of the article, they found the participants who set *audacious* goals were far more apt to like their job than those who set SMART goals. The problem with SMART goals is that SMART goals leave little room for the *passion*.

The article in *Forbes* also used the word audacious for big goals, and it fits perfectly. A goal does *not* have to be specific, measurable, attainable, relevant, and time-bound (although some will be and can still be audacious). There must be an emotional element to the goal for it to be compelling. My bodybuilding show is a good example. The goal is measurable and has a deadline, but to do my first bodybuilding show at sixty-five was definitely audacious.

A first-grade teacher named Crystal Jones received a class of kids whose skills were all over the board but mostly subpar for their age. She did an outstanding job of setting goals that were compelling for her students, and the results were stunning:

> At the beginning of the school year, she announced a goal for her class that she knew would captivate every student: By the end of this school year, you are going to be third graders. (Not literally, of course, but in the sense they would have third-grade skills.)
>
> The goal was tailor-made for the first-grade psyche. First graders know very well what third graders look like – they are bigger, smarter, and cooler...
>
> One of her first efforts was to cultivate a culture of learning in her classroom, calling her students "scholars" and asked them to address one another that way. When people visited her classroom, she introduced her class as a group of scholars and asked them to define the term for the guest. They would shout, "A scholar is someone who lives to learn and is good at it..."
>
> By springtime, the kids' test scores had reached second-grade level. So Jones threw a graduation ceremony right before spring break. For the rest of the year, the kids took great pleasure in referring to themselves as "second graders." And by the end of the year, over 90 [7]percent of the kids were reading at or above a third-grade level.
>
> These were some of the same kids who, nine months earlier, didn't know the alphabet.

How do you make being a *scholar* specific, measurable, attainable, relevant, and time-bound? What if they had tried to make their goal fit the parameters of a SMART goal? The goals set by this

---

[7]   Chip Heath and Dan Heath, *Switch*, 74–75.

teacher and her class were so compelling that they lit a fire under those kids and rocked their world forever.

What do the following dreams have in common: "I am independently wealthy," "I am physically strong," and "I have powerful human relationships"? There is no ceiling on these dreams; they are practically limitless. You will be building on, and refining, those goals all your life. You will find that you will often exceed your wildest hopes and expectations, and then keep growing from there. Do not reduce a dream so it can be measured. Audacious goals have infinite possibilities, and so do you. Here are a few tips on setting goals:

- Put your goals in writing. Napoleon Hill didn't say it first but has been quoted by motivators for nearly 100 years: "Reduce your plan to writing. The moment you do this, you will have given concrete form to the intangible."
- Write goals that inspire you.
- Simply state goals as if they are already a fact. Do not use phrases like "I will" or "I will try," or "I want to." For example, "I am wealthy," "I am educated," "I am a person of character," "I own a chain of dog food stores," "I am a Ph.D.," or "I own a beach house." Set bigger goals in weaker areas of life. There is no perfect balance, and life is always in flux, but aim for as much balance as you can.
- Do not set goals for other people, such as "my son is a doctor."
- Albert Einstein said, "Great spirits have always encountered violent opposition from mediocre minds." It will increase accountability if you share your goals with a few people, but only share your dreams, goals, aspirations, and hopes with people who believe in you and will applaud your success.

A sample of written goals:

Infinite Goals

1. I am lean and strong.
2. I have a rich spiritual life.

3. I have a warm, sexy, and companionable relationship.
4. I am a master of self-discipline.
5. I am self-educated.
6. I am a leader and an authority in my field.
7. I am independently wealthy.
8. I am a person of integrity.

Finite Goals

1. I climb Mt. Fuji.
2. I read the Qur'an.
3. I teach my children to ski.
4. I attend _____ seminar.
5. I read 52 books in one year.
6. I do three million in sales this year.
7. I leave a $100 tip.
8. I volunteer to serve at the homeless shelter.

ACTION STEPS

*"If you go to work on your goals, your goals will go to work on you.
If you go to work on your plan, your plan will go to work on you.
Whatever good things we build end up building us."*

~ Jim Rohn ~

Regardless of whether the goal is a *finite* goal or an *infinite* goal, it will require Action Steps. These are not the goal itself, but the specific steps needed to make the goal a reality. They are the day-to-day steps required, and the habits to be formed, to turn an audacious goal into a reality. The action steps alone are typically not very compelling because, unlike goals, they follow the SMART formula. They must be *specific, measurable, attainable, relevant, and time-bound.* While action steps alone are not compelling, when you see them as the means to acquiring your big, hairy, audacious goals, or as the means to acquire a result you are excited about, the enthusiasm to accomplish them increases. The examples below show the relationship between compelling goals and action steps:

- The goal "I am independently wealthy" is more compelling than "I invest $500 a month," but "I invest $500 a month" is an excellent action step.
- The goal "I have a loving, warm, companionable, and sexy marriage" is not measurable, but much more compelling than "I date my spouse once a week," but "I date my spouse once a week" is an excellent action step.
- The goal "I am lean and strong" is more compelling than "I train five days a week," but "I train five days a week" is an excellent action step.

A few tips on action steps:

- Plan action steps that will directly influence your goal.
- Write action steps in a language that inspires you.
- Strictly define what a completed action step requires. For example, can twenty pushups count as a workout in a pinch, or is completing a preset workout at the gym the only definition of a workout? Decide in advance, and then there is no question about whether you accomplished that action step.
- Ninety days is the golden timeframe for making change. Set action steps for ninety days, and every ninety days, reevaluate and reset for the next ninety days.
- Set your goals and action steps for each ninety-day period to be big enough to be exciting but not so big you are overwhelmed. If you unfailingly accomplish every action step, then you have set your goals too low. If you are missing over 25% of your action steps, then you have set them too high or not committed enough. If you consistently miss an action step or all the action steps for a certain goal, then you

may want to reexamine your commitment to it. Perhaps you will be more committed to it at a later date.

A sample of written goals with Action Steps:

Infinite Goals	Action Steps
1. I am lean and strong	1. I strength train 3x/week
	2. I do cardio 3x/week
	3. I eat clean—no bread or processed food
	4. I drink 80 oz of water daily
2. I have a rich spiritual life	1. I study my spiritual beliefs daily
	2. I write in a journal daily
	3. I attend church 4x/month
3. I have a warm, sexy and companionable relationship	1. I date _____ weekly
	2. I listen with sincere interest
	3. I take a weekend trip with ___
4. I am a master of self-discipline	1. I read motivational material daily
	2. I track my daily and weekly goals
5. I am self-educated	1. I read 20 minutes daily
	2. I attend one educational event
	3. I listen to educational material while driving to work
6. I am a leader and an authority in my field	1. I spend 30 minutes of my workday reading the latest information in my field
7. I am independently wealthy	1. I hire an investment professional
	2. I invest $500 a month
	3. I pay $500 a month toward debt

8. I am a woman/man of integrity	1. I am honest in every dealing
	2. I keep promises

Finite goals

1. I climb Mt. Fuji	1. I pick a date for Fuji
	2. I buy airfare to japan
	3. I train by hiking two hours 3x/week
2. I read the Qur'an	1. I read 6.5 pages of the Qur'an daily
3. I teach my children to ski	1. I buy a family ski pass
	2. I rent skis for the season
	3. I buy ski wear for each child
	4. We ski every Saturday
4. I attend ____ seminar	1. I purchase a ticket to __ seminar
	2. I clear my calendar for seminar dates
5. I read 30 books in one year	1. I make a list of 30 books to read
	2. I pick 10 books for the current 90 days
	3. I read 30 minutes daily
6. I do three million in sales this year	1. I increase sales by adding two sales calls a day
	2. I cut overhead by 5%
	3. I raise prices by 2%
	4. I attend a networking event weekly
7. I leave a server $100 tip	1. I leave a server $100 tip

8. I volunteer at the
   homeless shelter

1. I call the homeless shelter to learn about the needs at the shelter
2. I plan a date to serve
3. I organize the people and materials needed

Once your Action Steps have been committed to writing, each of them will need a plan for implementing them.

12

SYSTEMS

*"You do not rise to the level of your goals.
You fall to the level of your systems."*

~ James Clear ~

Every January, scores of people set New Year's resolutions in a determination to develop new habits. The problem with most New Year's resolutions is not that they aren't sincerely made, but that they are made without a system to support the goals. The goals are quickly lost sight of as other activities demand our attention. If you have set goals and failed to reach them, the problem is more likely the lack of a system for implementing those goals than a lack of self-discipline.

This lack of systems is the weak place in the goal-setting process, the place where it can all fall apart. Every Action Step of every goal must be recorded, implemented, tracked, and the progress measured. Once you have decided on your goals, which action steps you will take for the next ninety days, and have committed them to writing, then it is time to put systems in place. These systems will assist you in accomplishing your current goals and in establishing the life-long habits essential to personal growth. Systems are like a steam engine. As long you keep the engine moving, it will unfailingly move you forward. Apply one or more of the following systems to every action step:

- Daily Tracking Sheet
- Daily Written Affirmations
- Satisfaction Checklist

DAILY TRACKING SHEETS

"What gets measured gets improved."

~ Peter Drucker ~

The chart I set up when I was a young mother was what is now referred to as a tracking sheet. The idea came to me from mothers who made chore charts for their children. I thought, *If charts work for children to develop good habits, then why not me?* I started with three daily habits I wanted in my life but was struggling with consistency. I wrote these in the vertical column, then I wrote the days of the month across the top. It took time to make it a habit, but I have been doing those three items every day for forty years. I have no need to track them, and accomplishing them takes little of my precious daily allotment of self-discipline. I still use tracking sheets and currently have twelve daily items, plus a few weekly and monthly items.

To develop habits, things that we want to *do* on a daily, weekly, or monthly basis, there is no better system for self-accountability, tracking, and measuring than tracking sheets. Tracking sheets do the following:

- They keep you honest with yourself. When you track your activity, you can see exactly how you are doing, and there is no fooling yourself.
- It provides motivation and accountability. Knowing that you have to mark your chart at the end of the day can be enough to make you take action when you are tempted not to.

Tips for tracking:

- Write the items you wish to track as if it already is currently a fact. For example, "I read 15 minutes" or "I exercise daily" rather than "I *will* read 15 minutes" or "I *want* to exercise daily." You can also simply write, "read 15 min" or even "read" or "exercise" as long as you know precisely what that means.

- Be very clear about what qualifies as completed for each item. I once worked with a delightful but very obese young woman. She committed to daily workouts on her own on the days she wasn't working with me, but she missed frequently. Once, as we reviewed the previous week, she sheepishly asked if she could count walking from the parking garage to the restaurant, where she had dinner with her husband, as her daily walk. That short walk was just life happening, not her workout, and certainly not a step in the development of a new habit.

- Use a checkmark to identify things you have completed. When a certain item is not required that day, use an X. I learned the hard way that I need a day off from intense exercise, so I take Sundays off. On Sundays, I get an X. If your intention is to do a certain thing, and you neglect to do it, leave the box blank. This is very important. Our brain, or perhaps it's our ego, hates that empty box, but it also likes the feeling of checking something off.

- Mark it every day. You may even make that a tracking item: "I mark my tracking sheet daily." Keep your tracking sheet with you, in your planner, or on your pillow. Checking the items off as you do them is best, but definitely check your tracking sheet before you go to bed, and don't go to bed until you do. It also might inspire you to do something you might not otherwise do.

- You can also track weekly and monthly goals. If you use the tracking sheets free to you on my website, you will see a place for weekly goals and monthly goals.

When you look at the things you have planned for yourself, you should feel somewhere between excited and overwhelmed. If you get every check every time, then it is too easy. If you always fall short, then it is too hard. In that case, put it aside for now. You have your whole life to work on these things.

I had a charming client who set a goal to practice the piano every day. This was a skill that had lapsed, and she wanted it back—or so she thought. Each week she would recommit, but the weeks we met together, she had rarely practiced. I finally asked if she really wanted to practice. She replied she didn't think so. This experience is common. Sometimes we mix up what we really want with what we think we should want, or with what we once wanted, but have lost the interest.

If you are consistently missing something, then you may want to reevaluate, but be careful not to give up something you want just because it is hard. I have recently fallen in love with meditation. My goal is twenty minutes a day. I miss frequently. I have reevaluated and decided it is too valuable to me to quit. I tried less time, but then the meditation didn't feel as impactful. I considered fewer days a week, but I believe I need it every day. It's a challenge, but I am good at developing new habits and have decided I am up for the challenge, so I keep working on it.

Tracking is a great tool to teach your children. Our children learned this, and as adults, most of them practice it. Do not use bribery or rewards for your children or for yourself for meeting goals or completing a tracking sheet. Outside motivation won't work in the long term because when there is no longer a carrot, there is no longer incentive. Teach them to value the satisfaction of accomplishment over external reward. For more on this topic, I would recommend the book *Drive* by Daniel Pink.

Below is a list of the items I wanted to track and a re-creation of my tracking sheet for the month prior to submission of this book for publishing and included as an afterthought. It represents an average month for me.

Daily

Planning my day/Affirmations

Morning pages (three written pages as per Julia Cameron in *The Artist's Way*)

Meditate 20 min

Scripture study and memorization

Journal entry

Read

Review monthly/yearly goals

14,000 steps

Workout (4x/week)

50 pushups or 100 crunches or 3-minute plank

70 ounces water

Make a phone call

Monthly

Two new things

Accomplish 95% of daily habits

(I didn't have any weekly goals this month)

Daily Tracking

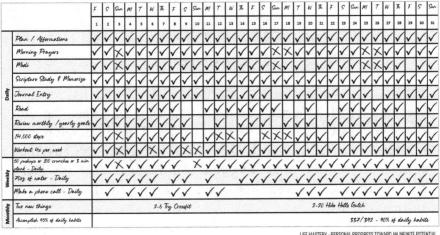

Planning my day, affirmations, scripture study and memorization, workouts, and journal writing are solid habits and have been for years. These items are non-negotiable even if I am traveling. I still track them as a reminder that even though I am struggling in some areas, there is still much I am accomplishing, and it gives my day momentum. Reading daily and getting 14,000 steps a day is typically pretty solid, but I missed a few times this month. Drinking enough water is a constant struggle for me even though I have been working on that for a long time, but I do better when I track it, so I keep plugging along. I added a daily phone call this month because I hate making phone calls, and I think it's time to get over it. You can see that I am still resisting making phone calls. I am including phone calls again this month and fully intend to do better. I had minor surgery the last week of the month and could not do some of the physical things, and those activities received an X. I have been practicing the development of habits for decades and can manage quite a few. If you are new to tracking daily habits, do not add too many too fast.

You can download tracking sheets in various sizes at LifeMasteryInfo.com

DAILY WRITTEN AFFIRMATIONS

"Language creates reality."

~ Deepak Chopra ~

Keeping a tracking sheet is an outstanding habit for developing habits and works well for things we want to *do* and for the development of habits. When we have goals to *be* something or on occasions when we want to work on something that is difficult to measure, Daily Written Affirmations work best. Here are some ways Daily Written Affirmations are useful:

- The development of characteristics. Things we want to *be* rather than *do*. When I told my staff at FitMania that I wrote *I laugh easily and often* in my affirmations, my sweet assistant said, "Why? You laugh a lot!" It is true. I laugh easily and often now, but I wrote that affirmation for several years before they knew me. I still write it in some form every day because I want to continue to improve, and I do not want to lose the progress I have made.

- Affirmations are where we put those things that cannot be decisively measured. Do you want to be a better listener? Love harder? Be more joyful or grateful? More kind?

- Staying focused on certain problems in order to solve them is another use of Daily Written Affirmations. A man signed up for coaching with me. We did the assessment and, over the course of the next few weeks, discussed his life and his goals. He had work to do in several areas, but what was most on his mind were issues at work. When I introduced him to Daily Written Affirmations, it resonated with him. After that session, he disappeared for several weeks. When he finally made it back, he was more animated than I had ever seen him. He had solved the problems at work, plus a few other issues, through the use of Daily Written Affirmations. He felt like this practice alone was worth all he paid me and was all he needed for future development. I hope he will be back someday. I think I have a few more things to teach him. But he was happy for now because *personal progress toward an infinite potential is the key to happiness.*

- Another use of Daily Written Affirmations is in the attainment of something you want, but you can find no viable course of action to acquire it, or possible action steps seem too limited. When I was looking for an effective way to get more education faster, I wrote in my affirmations *I am self-educated.* I had no idea how that might be accomplished, but I wrote that affirmation daily. After a few months, a friend found a flyer from Great Courses in his mailbox and gave it to me. Neither of us had heard of Great Courses at that time. He wasn't interested but said he thought of me when he saw it. He had no idea I was looking for something. The success I have found with this program has been incredible! My personal growth accelerated in every area of my life. Sometimes uncanny, almost magical things have happened.

- The way affirmations can be helpful is to reinforce an action step. If you have a goal to train five days a week, you might include an affirmation such as "I am strong and fit." You can even be more direct if it works better for you. For example, you could put "I train daily Monday through Friday" or "I train M-F" on your tracking sheet.

As you try this program, miracles will happen in your life. Often it will be because you consciously, or unconsciously, focused on your goal, and other times it will seem as if supernatural forces are at work. You may have no idea how a certain affirmation will be accomplished but go ahead and write it anyway. These are often the ones where miracles happen. Or perhaps it is simply that *what you think about expands*. Here are a few sample affirmations to get you started:

I am exuberantly happy
I have excellent posture
I listen sincerely
I speak well of others
I am at peace with myself and my peers
I work well with my team
I solve _____ issue with my staff
I am patient as my child learns _____
I own my own business
I find a loving life companion

Here are a few tips for effective daily affirmations:

- In a spiral notebook, or your day planner, if you use one, write your five to twelve most important affirmations. If you have less than five, it may not feel worth the effort. More than twelve, and it might feel too overwhelming.

- Use powerful adjectives. Write them in language that gets you excited.
- Once you have refined your affirmations, write them from memory.
- Write your affirmations as if you have already accomplished them. "I have excellent posture" or "I am a good listener."
- Always write them in the positive. Write "I am financially independent" rather than "I am debt-free."
- Write them every day. Missing even one day will set you back. If you want results, you must be absolutely consistent.
- Occasionally, a goal might fit well with both tracking and affirmations. Pick which one feels like it will get you the best results, or do both.
- For double accountability in keeping a tracking sheet consistently and writing Daily Affirmations consistently, add *I write my affirmations daily* to your tracking sheet and *I use a tracking sheet daily* to your Daily Written Affirmations.

After the first few weeks, this process will only take you a couple of minutes at most. This small investment of time will yield a gigantic impact on your life.

SATISFACTION CHECKLIST

The Satisfaction Checklist is fun—at least I think it is fun. This is where everything you want to accomplish is recorded. A Satisfaction Checklist is random because it can include both planned goals, planned action steps, and anything you happen to accomplish during the ninety days that were not in your written goals but in which you take pride for accomplishing. It is also focused because each item must be measurable and attained in the current ninety-day period. Writing, refining goals, and practicing habits is hard work, and by necessity, there is a lot of focus on what isn't getting done. You will have times where you wonder if you have accomplished anything at all, but when you see all you have accomplished in ninety days, you will hardly be able to wait to start on the next ninety days! Your Satisfaction Checklist covers the same ninety-day period as your goals and includes the following:

- Each *finite* goal.
- Any action steps you will be particularly pleased to have accomplished, or that need extra accountability.
- Items from your Big Dreams list you may happen to accomplish.
- Any difficult thing you accomplish of which you are proud.

This list is random and fun, but also critically important. It will keep you motivated, give you a sense of satisfaction for all you have accomplished, and most importantly, will be a permanent record of ninety days of personal growth. Here are a few tips to get you started on your own Satisfaction Checklist:

- Goals, action steps, and any other thing you do that makes you proud during the ninety days can be listed.
- Every item is measurable, and you must have a clear sense of what it means to complete an item. Either you did it, or you didn't do it. Don't leave room to waffle.
- Each item is intended to be done within the ninety-day period.
- If you have a goal to do several similar things, list them separately. For example, rather than write, *I will read four books* list each book as a separate item. Write 1. "Read *War and Peace,*" 2. "Read *The Compound Effect,*" 3. "Read *Life Mastery: Personal Progress Toward an Infinite Potential,*" 4. "Read *Frankenstein.*" If you haven't decided which books to read yet write "Read _____" for each book and fill it in when you decide.
- If you include items from your Daily Tracking sheet, break them down into small chunks of time. For example, if you have "I read to my children every night" as a daily item, instead of writing "I read to my children every night for ninety days,"

write "I read to my children every night for thirty days" and write it three times. This way, if you miss one day, you haven't lost the goal for the entire goal-setting period. It gives you room to start again and enjoy the sense of accomplishment filling the goal will bring. If you are struggling with an item, try breaking it down into twelve one-week goals.

- To ensure you are enjoying the full benefit of the list, review it at least weekly. Write "I read my Satisfaction Checklist" as a daily or weekly item on your Daily Tracking sheet.

- There is no limit to the number of items you list, but the list should be bold enough to inspire you, and short enough to prevent swamping you. At the end of the ninety days, if you accomplish 75% of the items, that is a good ninety days of work! What you do not accomplish can be added to the next period.

- Don't worry about writing the list in any particular order, or whether an item is appropriate. The goal-setting process is fluid. Add items or delete them throughout the ninety days as they fit your own aspirations.

- Keep your Satisfaction Checklist in a notebook or journal. At the beginning of each ninety days, write a journal entry about your hopes and feelings for the next ninety days. At the end, write another entry regarding your thoughts and feelings about the last ninety. This is something I wish I had started earlier. What a marvelous record of accomplishments you will have if you do this faithfully over your lifetime.

- Celebrate the victory of each item you check off.

SAMPLE OF A SATISFACTION CHECKLIST

1. I train five times a week for 30 days.
2. I train five times a week for 30 days.
3. I train five times a week for 30 days.
4. I hike Lucky Peak Mountain.
5. I take swim lessons.

6. I attend one seminar in my field.
7. I read *The Road to Character*.
8. I read *Tao Te Ching*.
9. I read _____.
10. I read _____.
11. I visit Aunt Martha.
12. I run a marathon.
13. I have a program for marathon training.
14. I have a coach for marathon training.
15. I join a networking group.
16. I develop a podcast on _____.
17. I put $2,000 in savings.
18. I try three new restaurants.
19. I write my Governing Values.
20. I keep a Daily Tracking sheet.

You will have items on your Satisfaction Checklist, your Affirmations, and even your Tracking Sheet that are not necessarily an action step. But every Action Step must be plugged into one at least one of these systems. Using the same sample goals, I have indicated what, in most cases, would be the best possible options for each action step:

INFINITE GOALS	ACTION STEPS	SYSTEM
1. I AM LEAN AND STRONG	1. I STRENGTH TRAIN 3X/WEEK	TS
	2. I DO CARDIO 3X/WEEK	TS
	3. I EAT CLEAN – NO BREAD OR PROCESSED FOOD	TS / AFFIRMATION
	4. I DRINK 80 OZ OF WATER DAILY	TS
2. I HAVE A RICH SPIRITUAL LIFE	1. I STUDY MY SPIRITUAL BELIEFS DAILY	TS
	2. I WRITE IN A JOURNAL DAILY	TS
	3. I ATTEND CHURCH 4X/MONTH	TS / SC

LIFE MASTERY

3. I HAVE A WARM, SEXY, AND COMPANIONABLE RELATIONSHIP	1. I DATE _____ WEEKLY	TS / SC
	2. I LISTEN WITH SINCERE INTEREST	AFFIRMATION
	3. I TAKE A WEEKEND TRIP WITH ___	TS / SC

| 4. I AM A MASTER OF SELF-DISCIPLINE | 1. I READ MOTIVATIONAL MATERIAL DAILY | TS |
| | 2. I TRACK MY DAILY AND WEEKLY GOALS | TS / AFFIRMATION |

5. I AM SELF-EDUCATED	1. I READ 20 MINUTES DAILY	TS
	2. I ATTEND ONE EDUCATIONAL EVENT	TS / SC
	3. I LISTEN TO EDUCATIONAL MATERIAL WHILE DRIVING TO WORK	TS

| 6. I AM A LEADER AND AN AUTHORITY | 1. I SPEND 30 MINUTES OF MY WORKDAY READING THE IN MY FIELD LATEST INFORMATION IN MY FIELD | TS |

7. I AM INDEPENDENTLY WEALTHY	1. I HIRE AN INVESTMENT PROFESSIONAL	SC
	2. I INVEST $500 A MONTH	TS / SC
	3. I PAY $500 A MONTH TOWARD DEBT	TS / SC

| 8. I AM A WOMAN/MAN OF INTEGRITY | 1. I AM HONEST IN EVERY DEALING | AFFIRMATION |
| | 2. I KEEP MY PROMISES | AFFIRMATION |

FINITE GOALS

1. I CLIMB MT. FUJI	1. I PICK A DATE FOR FUJI	SC
	2. I BUY AIRFARE TO JAPAN	SC
	3. I TRAIN BY HIKING TWO HOURS 3X/WEEK	TS

| 2. I READ THE QUR'AN | 1. I READ 6.5 PAGES OF THE QUR'AN DAILY | TS |

| 3. I TEACH MY CHILDREN TO SKI | 1. I BUY A FAMILY SKI PASS | SC |
| | 2. I RENT SKIS FOR THE SEASON | SC |

205

		3.	I BUY SKI WEAR FOR EACH CHILD	SC
		4.	WE SKI EVERY SATURDAY	TS
4.	I ATTEND ____ SEMINAR	1.	I PURCHASE A TICKET TO ____ SEMINAR	SC
		2.	I CLEAR MY CALENDAR FOR SEMINAR DATES	SC
5.	I READ 30 BOOKS IN ONE YEAR	1.	I MAKE A LIST OF 30 BOOKS TO READ	SC
		2.	I PICK 10 BOOKS FOR CURRENT 90 DAYS	SC
		3.	I READ 30 MINUTES DAILY	TS
6.	I DO THREE MILLION IN SALES THIS YEAR	1	I INCREASE SALES BY ADDING TWO SALES CALLS A DAY	TS
		2.	I CUT OVERHEAD BY 5%	SC
		3.	I RAISE PRICES BY 2%	SC
		4.	I ATTEND A NETWORKING EVENT WEEKLY	TS
7.	I LEAVE A SERVER $100 TIP	1.	I LEAVE A SERVER $100 TIP	SC
8.	I VOLUNTEER AT THE HOMELESS SHELTER	1.	I CALL THE HOMELESS SHELTER TO CHECK THE NEEDS AT THE SHELTER	SC
		2.	I PLAN A DATE TO SERVE	SC
		3.	I ORGANIZE THE PEOPLE AND MATERIALS	SC

13

HABIT

"For the ordinary business of life, an ounce of habit is worth a pound of intellect."

~ Thomas B. Reed ~

O ut of curiosity, I recently typed "daily habits for success" in my search engine. There were several pages of results, and many of them suggested a certain number of required habits for a successful life. The number of habits needed varied from one article to the next, such as *5 Habits to a Successful Life*, *25 Habits of Successful People*, or *100 Success Habits*, and one article suggested 203 habits that are necessary for success. How many daily habits are necessary, and what are they? While there are certainly some types of habits that every successful person needs to develop, such as fitness or study, the habits you develop and the number of those habits depend on what you want to accomplish and, more importantly, who you are trying to become.

Instead of brushing your teeth twice a day, would you consider saving time by brushing them once a week, fourteen times as long, with fourteen times the amount of toothpaste? How effective would it be to take a handful of vitamins occasionally, rather than make the effort to remember to take one every day? Would practicing the violin seven hours on your day off replace the daily habit of practice?

These are all ludicrous, of course. It is the *daily* habit that makes the practice effective.

Is it any less absurd to work hard every day to get in great shape and, having met your goal, quit the habits that created your success? How about putting money in a retirement account faithfully for a few years and then quitting the habit because money is tight one month? And yet, for some reason establishing a habit long enough to see a result and then abandoning the habit is a common failing in personal development. Habits must be constantly refined and built upon for lifelong progress and maintained over a lifetime. Success comes when small things are done consistently over time.

Successful people form habits out of the things less successful people won't do consistently. They like the results they get by doing what they don't always enjoy. The success you find in every area of Life Mastery will be a direct result of the habits you develop. It is truly as F.M. Alexander said: "People do not decide their futures, they decide their habits, and their habits decide their futures."

YOU ARE THE CURE

"Character is the ability to carry out a good resolution long after the excitement of the moment is passed."

~ Cavett Roberts ~

Many years ago, I heard Wayne Dyer tell a story I did not understand at the time. The story was about a Thai policeman who was encouraged by his mother, who was a monk of some kind, to help heroin addicts instead of arresting them. The policeman went to a monastery and practiced the austerities that the monks practiced. I don't remember much about what those austerities were, but sleeping on a bed of nails comes to mind. Instead of practicing a limited number of these austerities, as the monks did, he practiced them all. Once he had mastered these disciplines, he set off for Bangkok to collect heroin addicts who wanted a second chance. He then hauled them in the back of a truck to the monastery where, in front of these addicts, he injected himself with heroin. The heroin had no obvious effect, and then he said to them (and this is what I didn't understand at the time), "I am the cure."

I was intrigued, but I also wondered what the point was and why the policeman did not become addicted. And then, one day, I found myself saying the same thing—in my own mind. My problem wasn't heroin. It was sugar. I have always loved fancy desserts. I baked a lot when my children were home, and when I went out for dinner, I didn't feel satisfied until I had a dessert. And I was rarely interested in sharing one. This *addiction* to sugar—and it is an addiction—was not consistent with the image I had of myself and who I wanted to be. It wasn't a question of weight control but self-control. So I gave up processed sugar. Period. I was sugar-free for perhaps a year when I attended a nice buffet dinner with a table of beautiful desserts. As I walked by that table, I felt no temptation at all. I could eat one, or not, but it would be completely my choice. Now when I pass up a cookie or dessert, I get comments like "you are so good" or "you can cheat a little." I am not being "good" or "not cheating" (both are phrases I despise when it relates to food). It is now who I am. I am a person who doesn't eat every sweet thing that comes my way. I didn't need to count Weight Watcher points or be hypnotized or any other program outside myself. The answer came from my inner self.

A few years later, after chasing down outward programs like chiropractors, doctors, creams, and pills, I solved chronic pain issues internally. In both these instances, I found myself saying, "I am the cure," and I have a better understanding of the story about the Thai policeman. This man had developed self-discipline, self-understanding, and inner strength to the point he had ultimate control of his physical self. The power he developed over himself gave him the strength to lift people whose situation would other-wise have been hopeless. As your inner self is strengthened, you will frequently find that answers to problems will come from the inside rather than external sources. The stronger you become, the more you will realize that *you are the cure*. And how is that kind of strength gained? It is by absolute consistency to daily habits that are built and then continually refined. It is by what you do every day. It is the daily habits that we accumulate over our lifetime.

Turning down a piece of cake today is nice, but it won't amount to much on its own. Turning down desserts every day for the rest of your life has a big payoff. Reading for thirty minutes today is nice, and may be helpful, but reading thirty minutes every day for a year? Ten years? A lifetime? What kind of difference does that make? Whether it is taking your vitamins, flossing your teeth, making a set number of sales calls, training, reading to your kids, or a myriad of other things, it is the *consistency* that will make a difference. It isn't just an accumulative effect. These habits don't just accumulate, but like compound interest, each habit builds on itself, and the habits build on each other. Darren Hardy calls it the compound effect.

I have referred several times to a hiking trip we took with Brady (the fifteen-year-old son of our daughter Sarah), our daughter Summer, and my sister Jamie. I have had a lot of opportunities to travel. I have been to all seven continents and over forty countries. I have experienced many of the wonders of this world, but this hiking trip was easily the most life-changing. The Tour du Mont Blanc was ten vigorous hiking days in the Alps. Every day we climbed a different mountain and hiked down the other side. As we hiked, we traveled through France, Italy, Switzerland, and back to France. Every day, that day's hike seemed daunting, but every day we made it. And every day, we got up and did it again without discussion. Every day we each did what needed to be done without hesitation. One day it was raining so hard that many hikers took a bus to the next stop, but we hiked. Every day was hard, but every day was also a joyous journey. On the last day, we looked back at all we had done, and all we had learned, by simply putting one foot in front of the other all day long, every day. That journey was harder than any of us expected, but we were all stronger and more capable than we knew we were. Not one of the five of us will ever be the same. We experienced the perfect real-life metaphor of the compound effect of continually putting one foot in front of the other until we met our goal. (Our adventure was beautifully recorded and available at https://youtu.be/XZmHMZdt8jE)

THE HABIT PROCESS

"Both success and failure are largely the results of habit!"

~ Napoleon Hill ~

We each have a limited amount of self-discipline every day. It is like a daily savings account. Every time we have to push ourselves to do a thing that needs doing or prevent ourselves from doing a thing we ought not to do, we make a withdrawal. However, once something has become a well-established habit, or a bad habit has been broken, it takes little of our precious discipline. It also leaves ample self-discipline in our account to work on the next habit to be developed. The development of a new habit goes through three stages:

Honeymoon phase. In the honeymoon phase, you will be excited about your new goal and the vision you have of what you will achieve. You see fat investment portfolios, slender bodies, being the proprietor of your own business, a blissful family life, and so on. This phase is like being in love. You open doors for the beloved, make cookies, call to say, "I love you," and do so eagerly. Why? Because you are in love and have beautiful images of what your future will be.

Doldrum phase. The doldrum phase is the most important phase. It is also the most difficult. It's still love, but the newness has worn off. Now it takes effort and discipline to put on those running shoes or pick up that book. Baking cookies, holding a door, or making a phone call requires more concentrated effort, and there are times we simply do not want to do it. Even though we still want to have the habit and become the person we dream of being, there are many days when it just doesn't feel like it's worth it. This is the phase where most people quit. If you are 67% more likely to miss a second workout, the same may be said of other newly acquired habits. This is the phase where you remind yourself that *staying strong in the middle is a life skill.* It is so important to never miss because the more consistent you are during the doldrum phase, the less likely you are to quit, and the shorter the doldrum phase will last. As you push through the obstacles, you might discover what William James did. He said, "Beyond the very extreme of fatigue and distress, we may find amounts of ease and power we never dreamed ourselves to own; sources of strength never taxed at all because we never push through the obstruction."

If you are struggling through the doldrum phase, try upping your game in some way. If you have a running commitment and are struggling, then try a new route, buy some cool new shoes, or increase your speed or distance. If reading has become a drudgery, then look for ideas in the books you are reading that you like and underline them or find another book. If you are tired of saving, then put extra money in your account or give a few extra dollars to charity. If you are tired of your new commitment to eating better, then try a new recipe. If work has become a grind, then put more effort into your work attire and bring your colleagues a treat. I know that making a habit harder in order to bring back the enthusiasm is counterintuitive, but it works. You will generate enthusiasm for the goal and a boost in personal growth in the process. You will feel happier because *personal progress toward an infinite potential is the key to happiness.*

Another trick to get through the doldrum phase is to measure your progress. Remember how you felt when you started, and now see how far you have come. When we hiked the Tour Du Mont Blanc, we had to stay focused on putting one foot in front of the other hour after hour. That was important because we had to climb a mountain, get down the other side, and to our destination before dark. It was also important to stop, look down at the valley below us, and see how far we had come. Then look up at the magnificent Alps (and they were truly magnificent) and look ahead to see what still needed to be done. We did this often and instinctively. It was a crucial part of the marvelous experience of the Tour du Mont Blanc.

Become the cure. You will know you are entering the third phase, becoming the cure, when your habits become less about things you *do* and more about who you are *becoming*. You don't eat sugar, not because you are on a program but because you are a person who doesn't eat sugar. You are not training to get a beach body; you are a person who trains as a way of life. You are no longer working on being kind; you are a kind person. You are an avid reader, you live within your means, you are honest, and you have satisfying relationships. This is who you are, but you are not done. You will keep getting better at all these things and more because you have *become* a person who is always progressing.

14

ROADBLOCKS AND OPPORTUNITIES

*"The harder the conflict, the more glorious the triumph.
What we obtain too cheaply, we esteem too lightly."*

~ Thomas Paine ~

FIXED BELIEFS

*"The most important and most difficult thing that you can
change is your fixed false beliefs."*

~ Debasish Mridha ~

Remember the full-grown adult elephants tethered by a small rope tied around their back right leg? They are physically able to break the rope and go where they please, yet they stay tied to the spot. Their leg is fixed to the spot only because their minds have a fixed belief about what is possible. People also have fixed beliefs that limit their freedom to achieve them. We all have fixed beliefs, but only those who are willing to examine their thinking and challenge it can change it.

The footwear commonly known as flip-flops have been popular now for several decades. When they first debuted, I was a girl. Younger people snicker when I tell them it was originally called a thong. When the thong first came out, I tried a pair on and decided they weren't for me. I found the piece of rubber between my toes impossibly uncomfortable. When the thong disappeared and came back as flip-flops, I didn't try them because I already knew I couldn't wear them. I have had some unexpected, but needed, personal growth in recent years. There were things I thought to be true that turned out to be fixed beliefs. I have learned to ask myself, "What if that is not so?" That practice has opened my mind to some new ideas. So, recently when I was bemoaning how my options for summer shoes were limited by my inability to wear "flip-flop" styles, I asked myself the question, "What if that is not so?" I bought a pair and wear them often. All these years, I missed wearing so many great shoes because of a fixed belief!

Many of us have been conditioned to accept less than we can have and to be less than we can be. This is a common problem in fitness. Many people think being lean and strong is for other people. This self-limiting belief can slow or halt their efforts to be lean and strong. What have you been conditioned to believe about your body that might be holding you back? And while you are thinking about that, you might ask yourself the same question about your job and your relationships and any other places you might feel stuck. Every one of us can do more and be more than we think we can. Don't be held back by what you believe about yourself and your limitations. When you suspect your limitations are a result of fixed beliefs, ask yourself, "What if that isn't so?"

OBSTACLES

*"If you can find a path with no obstacles,
it probably doesn't lead anywhere."*

~ Frank A. Clark ~

Friedrich Nietzsche said, "That which does not kill us makes us stronger." Even though we usually quote him with an eye roll, he is right. Obstacles are not only an inevitable part of personal development; they are essential to the process. In the preface of his book *The Obstacle Is the Way*, Ryan Holiday quotes Marcus Aurelius: "The impediment to action advances action. What stands in the way becomes the way." Ryan then writes the following:

> "In Marcus's words is the secret to an art known as *turning obstacles upside down*. To act with 'a reverse clause,' so there is always a way out or another route to get to where you need to go. So that setbacks or problems are always expected and never permanent. Making certain that what impedes us can empower us."

A police officer, speaking to a group of women on how to protect themselves, explained how police officers who routinely go through possible emergency scenarios in training react better in an emergency, even if the particular scenario had never been practiced. Why? Because they learn how to anticipate emergencies and learn how to react to them with calm. If women think through how to react to various situations, it will improve their chance of protecting themselves from someone whose intent is to harm them. You will absolutely encounter obstacles in your path to your infinite potential. Apply this same principle in anticipating obstacles in the pursuit of your dreams. Know in advance there will be obstacles, and like the policemen in training, apply the principle of anticipating what obstacles you might encounter in advance, and how you will react to those obstacles. Practice keeping a calm mind and a clear focus when obstacles appear. Plan in advance to go around, through, or over obstacles. Decide in advance you will not have your dreams derailed by obstacles.

FAILURE

An artist who sells scenic paintings of the Northern California Coast was doing a demonstration of his method of painting to a small group. We watched as he painted a picture intended for sale. He finished the painting in about an hour and explained that, after a few touch-ups, the painting would sell for $1,500–$2,000. A young man in the group was stunned. He thought it unfair that the artist could earn so much money for only one hour of work. This talented man taught us all a lesson when he replied with good humor, "Before I sold paintings for $2,000, I spent thousands of hours painting hundreds of pictures that didn't sell at all. The buyers are paying me for those hours of practice as well as the painting." Sometimes you will fail, but failure is only permanent if you quit. Also, from *The Obstacle Is the Way*, Ryan Holiday wrote:

> "On the path to successful action, we will fail—possibly many times. And that's okay. It can be a good thing, even. Action and failure are two sides of the same coin. One doesn't come without the other. What breaks this critical connection down is when people stop acting—because they've taken failure the wrong way."

There will be obstacles, and there will be failure, but there is also power that comes when an individual has a dream and then calmly and persistently pursues that dream. Alexander Graham Bell had this to say about the power available to overcome both failure and obstacles: "What this power is I cannot say; all I know is that it exists, and it becomes available only when a man is in that state of mind in which he knows exactly what he wants and is fully determined not to quit until he finds it."

SUCCESS IS WHO YOU BECOME

Success is not a *doing* process, it is a *becoming* process, and we attract success by who we *become*. If you consistently set goals, achieve the goals you set, refine those goals, and set them again, then the pursuit of personal progress becomes who you are rather than something you do. You *become* an achiever who enjoys achievement and the happiness derived from personal progression. In the concluding pages of Phil Knight's book, *Shoe Dog,* he relates an experience. Knight was the founder of Nike. *Shoe Dog* is the story of the relentless pursuit of his dream to build a better running shoe, and a company to manufacture it. At the telling of this story, Knight was almost seventy years old and a billionaire. He had attended the movie *The Bucket List* with his wife. Knight had built one of the most well-known and successful companies in the world and accomplished many personal goals. He focused on specific causes and building projects at the University of Oregon. He gave an additional $100 million a year to charity. Still, the movie left him a little depressed and wondering if he had any dreams left. He wrote the following:

> "I can't sleep. I can't stop thinking about that blasted movie, *The Bucket List*. Lying in the dark, I ask myself again and again, What's on yours?
> Pyramids? Check.
> Himalayas? Check.
> Ganges? Check."

As he lays there thinking of things he might like to do, he begins to think about ways to tell his own story:

> "Another Crazy Idea.
> Suddenly my mind is racing. People I need to call, things I need to read…
> So much to do. So much to learn. So much I don't know about my own life.

Now I really can't sleep. I get up, grab a yellow legal pad from my
    desk. I go to the living room and sit in my recliner.
A feeling of stillness, of immense peace, comes over me.
I squint at the moon shining outside my window. The same moon
    that inspired the ancient Zen masters to worry about noth-
    ing. In the timeless, clarifying light of that moon, I begin to
    make a list."[8]

That is how Phil Knight happened to write *Shoe Dog*. He didn't
need the money or the fame. He needed a new dream and a new
goal. It's time to grab your own version of a yellow legal pad and
go to work!

- Block out a period of time where you will have no distractions
  or plan a retreat.
- Gather your answers to the reflection questions at the end of
  each chapter and the notes you have taken on ideas for goals,
  and a notebook for your deep reflection session.
- Take the assessment.
- Write or reflect on your Big Dreams list, Mission Statement,
  and Governing Values.
- Write your goals and action steps for the next ninety days.
  Do not wait on your Mission Statement or Governing Values
  if you haven't written them yet. Those take time and will
  come when you are ready.
- Apply every action step to a Daily Tracking Sheet, Daily
  Written Affirmations, or a Satisfaction Checklist.

---

[8] Phil Knight, *Shoe Dog* (New York: Scribner, 2016), 380–383.

CONCLUSION

There is an ancient story from the East about a lioness who was about to jump from one hillock to another when she gave birth to a cub. The cub fell down into the road where a herd of sheep was passing. The young cub fell among the sheep and began living with them. The young cub had no idea he was a lion. All around him were sheep and only sheep. He never roared like a lion because a sheep does not roar. He had never hunted alone like a lion because a sheep doesn't hunt and is never alone. He was always in the flock—cozy, secure, and safe. The cub eventually grew into a beautiful young lion. He looked different than the sheep, and sometimes behaved differently, but he was so used to thinking he was a sheep he never noticed. The sheep were so used to his odd behaviors that they didn't notice them. They continued to see him as one of their own and paid little attention to his uniqueness.

One day an old lion passed by and saw the young lion standing tall above the flock but grazing with the sheep. The old lion could not believe his eyes! The young lion even walked like a sheep. He had never seen such a thing! It was something so strange that he determined to catch hold of the young lion and find out what was happening. When the lion who thought he was a sheep realized he was being chased by a lion, he feared he would be eaten and ran for his life. When the old lion finally got hold of him, the younger animal cried and begged for his life, as a sheep would. The wise old lion took him to a nearby pond. The pond was silent, with no ripples, almost like a mirror. The old lion said, "Just look. Look at my face and look at your face. Look at my body and look at your body." As the sheep-lion began to see the truth, he let out a great roar! All the hills echoed with it. He had always been a lion, but now he knew it, and the world would know it, too.

ALLEGORY OF THE ELEVATOR

Using stairs instead of elevators, wherever possible, is a decision I made many years ago. At the time, it was an easy commitment to a small change in behavior. Three years ago, the commitment became much larger when we bought a condo on the top floor of the building. Six flights of stairs are tough anywhere, but there are over fifteen feet between floors; consequently, these six flights are particularly brutal. The door to the stairs is locked on the first floor, so accessing the stairwell requires taking the elevator to the second floor. Multiple times a day, I am faced with two choices. I can push the six and take a comfortable and quick ride home. In these moments, I hear the voice of our building manager, Dave, in my head when he asked me, "Why take the stairs when there is a perfectly good elevator available?" The other, harder choice, is that I can take the stairs. The benefits of taking the stairs any one time will be negligible to strengthening my body and my self-discipline, but what if I make the hard decision every time? Every day you are faced with little decisions. They will seem to be of little consequence in the moment, but they are like tiny threads that will be bundled together to determine what you achieve and who you become. Success comes by consistently pushing the two when you would rather push the six.

ACKNOWLEDGMENTS

Writing a book has been a marvelous experience and not one I ever anticipated having. It was the faith and confidence of the people around me—clients, coaches, and family—that encouraged me to write *Life Mastery*.

First and foremost among them is my husband, Ken, who is an excellent coach and mentor in his own right. He has supported me in every endeavor and has a unique ability to inspire me to fly higher than I thought possible and at the same time keep my feet on the ground. Ken proofread for me regularly as I wrote *Life Mastery* and would rave about how good the information is, tell me how badly people need this book, and how it would change lives. He was so sincerely enthusiastic that I knew he must be right. There were moments when I believed it only because he believed it.

The message of *Life Mastery* is clearer than it might have been because Summer Larson, our daughter, talked through the book with me at least three times and kindly kept me on course when I strayed. She also gave me the first glimpse of how infinite life's possibilities are forty-five years earlier.

My friend Robert "Rocky" Detweiler was my coach when I commenced this project. He told me I should write a book, and he believed I could do it. Rocky frequently refers to me as the "real deal." That comment played in my mind in moments of doubt.

When I began this book, I was coaching Leonardo "Lenny" Escobar. Lenny's enthusiasm for *Life Mastery* is so infectious that it kept me enthused and gave me a weekly opportunity to talk through many of the concepts.

Thank you to the teams at Authors Unite and Spitfire Creative for handling all the details, and making me look smarter than I am.

Immeasurable is the influence of the many prophets, philosophers, sages, and poets, both ancient and modern, at whose knees I have learned. They may not know me, but I know them, and I look forward to the day that I can thank them personally.

RECOMMENDED READING

A recommended reading list is a tricky thing to write because there are so many great books. In this case, I chose only books I have read thoroughly and have recommended regularly. Each of these books has impacted my life in tangible ways. I recommend them because I think they can influence yours. For updated versions of the Recommended Reading list visit LifeMasteryInfo.com.

Classics
As a Man Thinketh by James Allen
Think and Grow Rich by Napoleon Hill
How to Win Friends and Influence People by Dale Carnegie
The Strangest Secret by Earl Nightingale
The Power of Positive Thinking by Norman Vincent Peale
The Magic of Thinking Big by David J. Schwartz
The Greatest Salesman in the World by Og Mandino
The Richest Man in Babylon by George S. Clason
Man's Search for Meaning by Viktor Frankl
See You at the Top by Zig Ziglar
The 7 Habits of Highly Effective People by Stephen R. Covey

Goal Setting and Habit Development
The Compound Effect by Darren Hardy
Goals by Brian Tracy

The Slight Edge by Jeff Olson
The Power of Habit by Charles Duhigg
Atomic Habits by James Clear
The 10 Natural Laws of Successful Time and Life Management by Hyrum Smith

Motivation
The Day That Turns Your Life Around by Jim Rohn
The Art of Exceptional Living by Jim Rohn
Take Charge of Your Life by Jim Rohn
The One Thing by Gary Keller
Once Upon a Cow by Camilo Cruz
Who Moved My Cheese? by Spencer Johnson
The 4-Hour Work Week by Timothy Ferriss
Tribe of Mentors by Timothy Ferriss
Tools of the Titans by Timothy Ferriss
Eat That Frog by Brian Tracy
The Obstacle Is the Way by Ryan Holiday
Drive by Daniel H. Pink
The Road to Character by David Brooks

Money and Business
Rich Dad, Poor Dad by Robert Kiyosaki
Start with Why by Simon Sinek
The Infinite Game by Simon Sinek
The E-Myth by Michael E. Gerber
Deep Work by Cal Newport
Built to Last by James Collin and Jerry Porras

Relationships
Outliers by Malcolm Gladwell
The Five Love Languages by Gary Chapman
What Makes Love Last by John Gottman
His Needs, Her Needs by Willard F. Farley
The Kosher Sutra by Shmuley Boteach

Health

The Great Pain Deception by Steven Ray Ozanich
Rapid Recovery from Back and Neck Pain by Fred Amir
Live Long, Die Short by Roger Landry
The End of Alzheimer's by Dale Bredesen

9 781951 503420